Faith in Church Newspapers

*To John
In Solidarity
David
Lent 3
2025*

Faith in Church Newspapers

A Contextual Theology of Identifiable
Black Actors and "Race" Related Issues
Found in the *Church Times* and the
Church of England Newspaper

David Isiorho

WIPF & STOCK · Eugene, Oregon

FAITH IN CHURCH NEWSPAPERS
A Contextual Theology of Identifiable Black Actors and "Race" Related Issues Found in the *Church Times* and the *Church of England Newspaper*

Copyright © 2024 David Isiorho. All rights reserved. Except for brief quotations in critical publications or reviews, no part of this book may be reproduced in any manner without prior written permission from the publisher. Write: Permissions, Wipf and Stock Publishers, 199 W. 8th Ave., Suite 3, Eugene, OR 97401.

Wipf & Stock
An Imprint of Wipf and Stock Publishers
199 W. 8th Ave., Suite 3
Eugene, OR 97401

www.wipfandstock.com

PAPERBACK ISBN: 979-8-3852-1774-8
HARDCOVER ISBN: 979-8-3852-1775-5
EBOOK ISBN: 979-8-3852-1776-2

VERSION NUMBER 11/20/24

Scripture quotations are from the New Revised Standard Version Bible: Anglicised Edition, copyright © 1989, 1995 the Division of Christian Education of the National Council of the Churches of Christ in the United States of America. Used by permission. All rights reserved.

Polite Notice to Cold Callers

No politicians
No salespersons
No archdeacons

Contents

Acknowledgments | ix

Introduction: Why This Book? | 1

Chapter One
Identified and Identifiable Black Actors | 15

Chapter Two
"Race" Related Issues and Their Theology of Context | 30

Chapter Three
"Race," Ethnicity, and Black Theology | 56

Chapter Four
"Race," Ethnicity, and the Religious Press | 86

Conclusion: The Racialization Process and the Religious Press of the Church of England | 114

Appendix | 127
Bibliography | 131

Acknowledgments

To my beloved wife, Linda, who has encouraged me as an Anglican priest to do what Jesus did—challenge the institution and support the faith of the faithful. Linda shares my politics and theology and understands that *Faith in Church Newspapers* is just as much about the Church of England as it is the religious press.

I am grateful to Charlotte and Philip Swan, who led the retirement retreat at Shallowford House, UK, in July 2024. This time of reflection provided me with a quiet context in which to respond to that God-given inspiration I needed to complete this book and to acknowledge the prophetic act of witness I was engaged in.

Introduction

Why This Book?

I STARTED TO WRITE the introduction to *Faith in Church Newspapers* while on a retirement retreat. This time of reflection was professionally managed with a strong theological structure based on key themes from St. John's gospel.[1] The overarching theme was "Letting Go to Live Anew." I had an opportunity to reflect on where God had led me until now. In other words, how had I experienced God's love in my life and ministry focusing on my joys and regrets. I have for a number of years deliberately not over defined myself by my church function. So, the idea of letting go at an appropriate time my parochial position as rector or vicar of a particular church or place was not new to me or threatening. I have for some time perceived the prospect of retirement as a liberation process. However, there is a lot more to this retirement thing than letting go of a particular parochial position at a particular time and place. I have no issue with letting go of what I have been allowed to achieve, but what about those things I have never had an opportunity to aspire to?[2] That is a more difficult

1. See Ford, *Gospel of John*.
2. See Isiorho, *Mission, Anguish, and Defiance*, 43–48.

ask. When I was recommended for ordination training, I was told I would start off in a parish as an assistant curate and that this would be a launch pad to a senior post of responsibility. The selection secretary informed me that I would probably end up as a canon or dean of a cathedral somewhere. Well, here I am thirty-five years on about to retire with my impressive CV and none of the above has ever happened. This is a bereavement, experienced by many Black clergy, especially those born in the UK.[3]

I started to write another draft to this introduction having returned from a prestigious but disappointing rural ministry course. This made me wonder if the news items reported in *Faith in Church Newspapers* were going to be in a rural or urban context. I answer this question by exploring the historical, social, and political circumstances in which news items in church newspapers are constructed. Only then could I define the context. News items in the UK tend to be about urban situations where global majority heritage people are most likely to live and be subject to deprivation. However, having been a parish priest in rural settings as well as urban, I am all too aware that there is such a thing as rural poverty among farm laborers and tenants. We need a clearer focus here—a theme that would go beyond the obvious context to sharpen up our practice. Both rural and urban ministries identify discipleship in the context of a Christian presence in every UK community. So, to my mind, any division between these types of ministries must be based on the location and the financial wealth of significant participants to whom the church offers its ministry. I have to say that in my thirty-five years of parochial ministry, I have never met a poor farmer among those who own land and employ others on that land. For this reason alone, *Faith in Church Newspapers* will focus on urban theology issues, including the preferential option for the poor, because this is where research has been conducted that is relevant to this book.

---

3. See Isiorho, "Black Clergy Discontent," 221, 223–26.

Practical Theology

Research suggests that the mass media including newspapers can be held to some extent responsible for the continuation of racial stereotypes and myths that surround the concept of "race." The press can reproduce racism by framing the presence of non-White people in British society in terms of immigrant-host relationships. There is evidence that people from a global majority heritage are identified as a category in British society and portrayed as deviant. Their alleged traits, as well as being characteristic of their group, are also seen as the cause of many troubles affecting the majority culture. The first part of chapter 4 of *Faith in Church Newspapers* is based on my unpublished MA dissertation.[4] Having started this work at the beginning of my parochial ministry over three decades ago, I now complete this in the autumn. The second part of chapter 4 is a re-run of that research in contemporary times to find out if anything has changed in the religious press of the Church of England.

Faith in Church Newspapers offers a practical theology that looks at the way non-White people are portrayed in the religious press of the Church of England and have been racialized as *other than White*. The implicit starting point for this work is the contextual theology of the racialized other. This book is about the presence of God in those who can be identified in church newspapers as marginalized.

Faith in Church Newspapers is aimed at academics; church leaders; educationalists and racial justice activists in theological and higher education; diocesan social responsibility staff; all clergy and accredited lay workers undertaking or leading continuing ministerial education in the Church of England; and circuit ministers and local preachers in the Methodist and United Reform Church. This is an original book and one of crucial importance not just to Black histories and Black theology but also to urban and contextual theology. It would make a good textbook for theological

---

4. Isiorho, "Racialisation Process and the Religious Press."

students undertaking pastoral education and for students of journalism, history, and social change.

Urban Theology

I launched the research into the religious press of the Church of England over thirty-five years ago when I was an assistant curate at St. Mary's Abbey in Nuneaton, Warwickshire, UK. As a young curate, I embarked on three major life changes. I became a member of the Church of England clergy, started a master's degree in race and ethnic studies, and most importantly I married my wife, Linda. And talking about my wife, I have included her story as a brief case study of those marginalized as result of their marriage to a member of the global majority heritage. Linda and I have our own journeys of Christian witness, but many experiences have been shared. For example, we were in church late one Saturday afternoon in Bradford following a Black Christian meeting. The church door was open. Two tired people came in, a man and a woman. They were untidy and poorly dressed in flimsy shoes. It turned out that they had walked many miles to obtain some proof of the woman's identity so that she could claim certain benefits. They were temporarily lodged in a hostel in a town ten miles away. They had walked into Bradford and were now on their way back. They could not afford bus fare. Linda, my wife, washed the woman's feet that were sore and bleeding. Then we took them home and made sure that they were cared for. Both people had long histories of illness. Neither had ever been able to work. Each had long since lost any real home. But what they had not lost was the sense that the church was somehow their home. When they saw that open door, they felt sure that they were going to have some assistance. As Christians, we naturally think about those less fortunate than ourselves, or at least we should. I am thinking of those who are homeless and without much cheer at any time of the year, not just when the Christmas appeals arrive on our doorstep.

In his flesh, our Lord was no stranger to suffering and pain. He did not take the path of being different in condition from anyone else. He could have exercised his powers to float serenely through this vale of tears untroubled, but he chose not to. In his submission to the wounding that is the human condition, Jesus calls us to the same state. Our faith is not some kind of celestial insurance policy that wards off all the worst that life throws at us. Our faith is what enables us to face the world and to pray for it; not to turn away from anyone, however disgusting they may seem. The world depends on the steadiness of our gaze and the faithfulness of our prayers and actions.

And I started to think about what God's love for mortals means. God had taken our human nature and had added this to the divine nature. That is amazing and is why I am glad to be a Christian. But why did all this happen? According to Walter Bruggemann, it was because the people of the Old Testament cried out to God, and they were heard.[5] Their appeal to God for release from their oppression went to heaven and God took notice and responded to their cry. So, the ancient people of God thought it only right to make such a protest because they knew things were not right. *Faith in Church Newspapers* also cries out to God and is a prophetical act of witness. Bruggemann is very clear that in crying out to God, the people of the Old Testament were not looking for a quick fix and were only too aware that many of their concerns would be unresolved, but they would be faithfully waiting and hoping. So, we must ask the question, Who are we in our time to cry out to God and complain? The point being made is that if it is not felt right to pose the hard questions of justice directly to God, they soon appear also as improper questions to ask about our public institutions, including churches. All too often the order of the day is one of despair, and we give up. For Bruggemann, to cry out to God is to confess one's belief in a God who listens, a God who is in a relationship with you, a God who perhaps ultimately even suffers with you. However, if we are to cry out to God, then we must also join in with God taking sides with the poor and the oppressed, because our relationship with God is expressed in our relationship with the rest of humanity. Justice is tied up with holiness, and

---

5. Bruggemann, "Costly Loss of the Lament."

Jesus Christ is God become poor. We serve a demanding God who demands our participation in the creation of a just society.

Contextual Theology and Frame Analysis

Faith in Church Newspapers is about racialized imagery and racial bias to be found in two Church of England newspapers using the research tools of content analysis and frame analysis. *The Church Times* and *The Church of England Newspaper* contain implicit racialized beliefs about racial groups, and for that reason, these publications may be understood to be racially biased. The context in which identifiable global majority people and "race" related issues have been framed provides the conceptual map for the entire book.

The Church Times and *The Church of England Newspaper* were selected as the focus for this book because they are the main news publications of the Church of England. However, these papers claim to be independent of church authorities. It was felt that these two papers represented the bulk of church readership. My first sample comprises twelve copies of *The Church Times* and eleven copies of *The Church of England Newspaper*, which covered a period of three months, including December 1990 and January and February 1991. *The Church Times* and *The Church of England Newspaper* share the same publication date, that is the Friday of each week. However, there were only three editions of the *Church of England Newspaper* for December 1990, with one edition covering the twenty-first and twenty-eighth of that month. The time frame for our sample was determined in relation to the peculiarities that might be associated with that chosen. It included coverage of a General Synod. Furthermore, I felt that there would be more coverage of news issues during this period. My second sample comprises six copies of *The Church Times* and six copies of *The Church of England newspaper*, which covered a period of three months, including December 2023 and January and February 2024.

In the 1990–91 sample of both the *Church Times* and the *Church of England Newspaper*, only a minority of news items were concerned with "race" related issues or contained identifiable non-White characters. However, the percentage of these news items concerning identifiable Black and Asian people was greater in *The Church of England Newspaper* than in *The Church Times*, as was the percentage of these news items occurring in a context outside that of a "race" related problematic. In both publications, there was an avoidance of political issues involving Black and Asian people in Britain. The absence of non-White people was also found in the news items about non-White issues. There were more news items with White people discussing non-White issues than non-White people discussing those issues. In the *Church Times*, White people discuss non-White issues in the context of a predominantly White country, while in the *Church of England Newspaper*, they did this in the context of a predominantly non-White country. In the 1990–91 sample there was only one news item in which non-White characters discussed non-White issues in the context of a predominantly White country.

The findings show that the religious press of the Church of England contained a frame of reference that tended to exclude non-White people. When non-White actors did appear in the news items of these newspapers it was usually in a developing world context where they were the recipients of Western aid. The racialization process informs the way issues are structured in the press of the Church of England. This book is about not only excluding non-White people from the pages of church publications but also denying their presence in British society. When the presence of non-White people is acknowledged in church publications, it is seen in terms of immigrant-host relationships.[6]

In *Faith in Church Newspapers*, we will be concerned with the nature of ethnic inequalities and the power relationships between minority groups and the dominant culture in British society. I will try to understand how these structural inequalities have been racialized and reproduced through the religious press. This book will

6. Isiorho, "Black Identities and Faith Adherence," 292–94.

seek to clarify the pattern of representations to be found in these publications which convey racial prejudice and racism. The way issues are structured by the reporting process will be informed by the racialization process that operates in British society.

The religious press of the Church of England can reproduce racism by setting the agenda and affecting public reaction to events. This is manipulated by those who have access to its structures. These elite groups include politicians, professional media personnel, and influential people in the Church of England. However, the question always arises, Does this media create the social reality or merely reflect it? It could be claimed that even if it doesn't create the social reality, it reinforces attitudes already formed or in the process of formulation within the church.

The role of the religious press in the reproduction of racism cannot be seen in isolation from a racialization process that describes the role of Black and Asian people in British society in terms of "race"-dependent characteristics. These relationships are ideological and can be translated at the micro level into routines of news gathering. In this the religious press does not necessarily reflect racism or initiate it but, rather, as an institution in British society, must be seen as a participant in the racialization process.

My research has suggested that the religious press can be held to some extent responsible for the continuance of racial stereotypes and myths that surround the concept of "race" in the Church of England. The religious press supported by other mass media has reproduced racism by framing the presence of Black people in British society in terms of "race" related relationships. There is some evidence that Black people are identified as a category.[7] They, as well as being characteristic of their group, are also seen as the cause of many troubles affecting the majority culture. Black people are rarely blamed for illness without at least indirectly referenced to several others. At its extreme, the press has presented Black people as diseased muggers who rape defenseless White widows and come from promiscuous, unstable family backgrounds as well as being unemployed and high on drugs, to say nothing of having

---

7. Gaffney, *Interpretation of Violence*.

entered the country illegally to live in squalid housing. The religious press can criminalize the Black community and make that community appear deviant because the press reflects, expresses, and maintains a system of racism. So, is racism reproduced in church publications? To evaluate this, I have devised a system of empirical indicators to operationalize the concepts of racialization and racism. I also needed a set of criteria dealing with the contextual aspects of a racialization process. The following guidelines were tentatively suggested for examining the racialization process in *The Church Times* and the *Church of England Newspaper*.

- Is there a general absence of non-White people and issues relating to them?
- When non-White people and issues relating to them are being discussed, are all the contributors White?
- Are non-White people shown only in subordinate roles?
- Are White lifestyles portrayed as superior to non-White?
- Are non-White lifestyles depicted as primitive or heathen?
- Are hunger and poverty shown as non-White mismanagement?
- Are non-White people portrayed as objects of charity?
- Are events of history only considered from a European point of view?
- Are geographical factors stereotyped—is the developing world shown only as bush, referred to as barren, and reference made to a lack of White technology?
- Are all non-White people categorized as immigrants?

I started this research with the understanding that institutions tend to produce literature containing racialized frames of reference, even when those institutions are committed to racial equality. I also thought that the more evangelical the ecclesiology of Anglican newspapers, the more racialized its frame of reference was likely to be. This book employed the method of content analysis to measure the frequency and extent of the coverage of racial topics in a representative sample of the religious press of the Church of England. This research method was used to determine the manifest content of these documents by a systematic and quantitative analysis. However, my interpretation of the findings of the content analysis is heavily informed by frame analysis.

The racialized frames of reference to be found in *The Church Times* and *The Church of England Newspaper* reflect the attitudes and values of those who produced these publications, and the message they, intentionally or unintentionally, get across to their readership. As for the readers themselves, I can only speculate and draw inferences about whether these publications also reflect their attitudes and values. The data that was collected and analyzed consisted of news items structured according to the following criteria:

- The number of news items with explicit concern for "race" related issues.
- The number of news items with identifiable non-White people
  - in which the context is one of "race" relations.
  - in which the context is not one of "race" relations.
- The number of new items about non-White issues with no identifiable non-White people.

The above structure represents the formalized procedures for conducting a systematic identification of racialized frames of reference in *The Church Times* and in *The Church of England Newspaper*. The content analysis is based on the systematic classification of news items according to the contextualized categories of frame analysis. It is the frame of reference that allows readers of church publications to make sense of the racialized world in which they live. These frames of reference are how people interpret their experiences.

My content analysis was based on a systematic inclusion/exclusion of specified attributes of communication according to explicitly formal rules and procedures. I provide quantitative descriptions in the form of data that can be summarized and compared. These systematic classifications involve interpretation and, for this reason, I have set out the conditions under which data was collected. Although content analysis prides itself on the use of rigorous analytical and statistical procedures, it can never guarantee objectivity. I have made subjective decisions about what constitutes specified content as I define the categories I have used and the direction in which the book is going. I understand content analysis is about drawing inferences and that this is a precondition for summarizing the data. It is also a precondition for the recognition of patterns and relationships which will enable us to test out ideas concerning racialized frames of reference and to do this with quantifiable categories.

So, what about the frame analysis in *Faith in Church Newspapers*? The frame analysis is the systematic classification of the racialized frame of reference contained in church publications. We are not so much concerned here with whether news items are in themselves racist but the circumstances under which identifiable non-White actors and "race" related issues have been framed, that is, the context in which they have been placed. Thus, the frame of reference is the framework of interpretation that can be used by readers of church publications to make sense of their environment. The framing process represents a specialized form of agenda setting through which racialized meanings can be conveyed.

In seeking to measure and count news items, my first task was to determine what constituted a news item. News items had to be distinguished from features. It was possible to find the definition of news items within the publications themselves. Usually, there were indications, such as section headings at the top of the page. When there were no section headings it was possible to identify a news item by its similarity in style to other news items that did have section headings. Overall, there were more news items in *The Church of England Newspaper* than in *The Church Times*. Percentages were drawn up so that comparisons could be made between these publications and between the two sets of samples spanning thirty-three years.

I used one method of numeration in the calibration of the results, namely **the appearance/non-appearance of specified items**: this involved a search of *The Church Times* and *The Church of England Newspaper* for the appearance/non-appearance of news items about "race" related issues and identifiable non-White actors. The data coded in this way is presented numerically in table 1 (see appendix). I could have focused on the time/space allocation to specified items of content and measured in square centimeters the amount of news coverage given in *The Church Times* and *The Church of England Newspaper* to the subject categories of Britain, Europe, the developing world, and the rest of the world. I could have also measured the frequency of specified items of content.

Clearly, there are weaknesses in this method of content analysis, particularly concerning the appearance/non-appearance of specified items. No distinctions are made between the occurrence of content items appearing on the front page from those appearing elsewhere in these publications. But data presented does not tell us the rank order of "race" related issues and identifiable non-White actors in relation to other attributes. An alternative approach would be to provide a system of weighted categories and account for all the identifiable issues and actors. However, this would involve building into the content analysis frequency and intensity scales, which could entail difficult and complex coding procedures.

After careful consideration, I decided that it was not important to know whether identifiable non-White actors were mentioned more than once in any news item or that they could be given special prominence by where they appear in the publications. My frame analysis was not concerned with the internal layout of *The Church Times* and *The Church of England Newspaper*. I wanted to know whether "race" related issues and identifiable non-White actors had been racialized by a context that is external to these publications. It is more important to know whether identifiable non-White actors have been framed in the context of a predominantly non-White country than whether these actors appear on the front page. Thus, the focus of my research was to account for how people experience and make sense of their environment by identifying the external variables that determine that experience.

The method of content analysis that has been used in this book asks questions about the religious press of the Church of England and the racialization process that operates in British society. Content analysis, informed by frame analysis, identified racialized messages in *The Church Times* and *The Church of England Newspaper* via the framing process of these publications. I draw inferences about the sender and receiver of racialized messages, by identifying specific characteristics of these messages. However, the effectiveness of my content analysis was dependent upon the categories that it deployed. Thus, it could only deal with those categories that fall within the boundaries of its application.

So, three decades on. Has anything changed in the religious press of the Church of England, and what sort of hypothesis after thirty-three years can be formulated about *The Church Times* and *The Church of England Newspaper*? Have these papers changed in any way, and what about the relationship between them? These are the crucial questions for *Faith in Church Newspapers*. I started this book with some implicit hypotheses, and I now feel I should make these ideas more explicit. I want to abandon the "race" relations perspective of the immigrant-host model in favor of an approach which seeks the formation of a research problem based on a racialization problematic. So, what do I mean? Well, institutions tend to produce literature containing racialized frames of reference, even when those institutions are committed to racial equality. To understand how people of global majority heritage are "framed" in the religious press of the Church of England, we must move the focus of our analysis to the social processes which reproduce social institutions. The racialized relations of production within capitalist societies have always been economic. Following Eric Williams, we can say that slavery was an economic system of racially unclassified exploitation which only brought about racism when racial meaning was attached to it. Thus, racism did not cause slavery. A similar line of argument is taken up by Sivanandan, who informs us that capitalism requires racism not for racism's own sake, but for the sake of capital.[8] Black and Asian people in British society have limited access to the resources which wealth and favorable market position make possible. It follows therefore that any discussion of "race," ethnicity, and the media must consider the differential distribution of resources and political power. This can only be explained in terms of what is meant by a racialization process which operates not only in British society but also in the Church of England. I am talking here about an institutionalized church that is more concerned with promoting a notion of Englishness than proclaiming the universal Christian faith.

And what about our implicit hypotheses? Well, there are several possibilities here. It could be that the *Church Times* and the *Church of England Newspaper* continue to marginalize global majority people in the way that they have done for the last thirty-three years and that there is no significant change in the data. It could be that these newspapers have improved their coverage and that they are less discriminating. Let's hope that the religious press has not become worse in the way that it portrays non-White actors. The other possibility is that these papers are not so homogeneous as they were three decades ago. The religious press operates in a definite context which is part of a racialization process. Chapter 1 of *Faith in Church Newspapers* gives focus to identified and identifiable case studies of people of global majority heritage. Chapter 2 will consider the historical background and possible origin for news items with an explicit concern for "race" related issues.

---

8. Sivanandan, *Different Hunger.*

Chapter One

Identified and Identifiable Black Actors

Introduction

In the spring of 1997, a news item appeared in the national press about a row that had erupted between a team vicar and her superior.[1] In the Kings Norton Team Ministry, Birmingham, UK, the Rev. Eve Pitts, a Jamaican-born priest with full British citizenship, was demoted to the status of an assistant curate, a junior role in the Church of England. The team rector decided Eve was to be based with him at St. Nicholas and work directly under his supervision even though she was originally licensed to Druids Health, where she would have a considerable amount of autonomy.

So how did Eve Pitts provoke a high level of media coverage? The nation was on the edge of its seat anticipating a general election, and the media was desperate for a human-interest story. In a private conversation with my wife, Eve talked about four years of hell in this parochial situation. Later that week, with

---

1. Isiorho, "Black Clergy Discontent," 217.

typical Eve bravado, her telephone answering machine played the Bob Marley classic "Everything's Going to Be All Right." So, what had been going on? There had been a breakdown in the working relationships between the clergy, and the bishop called upon Eve to resign, but she refused to be victimized in this way. This prompted Nicholas Ball to write a letter to *The Church Times* to state publicly how well he and Eve had worked together during her time as his curate at Bartley Green. This relationship had been so clearly fruitful that Eve had even been invited back to her training college, Queen's, Birmingham, UK, to give a seminar with her senior to the final year ordinands about how to form a successful connection with one's training vicar. Depending on the person being interviewed about this *cause célèbre*, Eve was presented in the media either as a woman of warmth and sensitivity in pastoral ministry or as the opposite, a person of prickly and tense approach to life, anxious for her own esteem. Eve was featured on television and Ceefax and Teletext; her case was reported on radio and in local and national newspapers, including the church press, who also covered the matter.

The Rev. Eve Pitts was banned from preaching. This is a drastic measure, which is calculated to wound as well as silence a priest. It was indicative of the efficiency of Eve's preaching. Her style is open and ardent, Christ-centered with a prophetic edge. It is profoundly un-Anglican to gag clergy for doing what the priesthood demands because they are called to use their time and talents to explore the faith within their present generation. So, in this context the Church of England no longer had an imperative to comfort the afflicted and afflict the comfortable, as Tissa Balasuriya put it. Sometimes our very creativity will do either or both in a profound ministry of being. As the Church of England thrashes about in what some see as its death throes, it is harming individuals and their mission by restrictive measures and practices, but this can never throttle the voice of the Spirit. When control is a major priority, then the identification of those who are to be controlled becomes an issue. It is at this level that any external marker becomes pivotal such as recognized racial origin through skin color and gender identification, which are useful to the establishment.

In Eve Pitt's case, the late Reverend Prebendary Theo Samuel, speaking for the Association of Black Clergy, referred to unwitting racism and sexism as being significant factors. The church several decades on has yet to take on board the full meaning of institutionalized prejudices. At the time a senior and respected bishop remarked to my wife that he likes and supports Black people. What, all of them, Bishop? Get real. This can't be taken seriously. The next section of this chapter concerns two case studies in which priests were not supported by the Association of Black Clergy.

Linda's Story

Our first case study in global majority heritage is that of my wife, Linda, a White woman, British-born, aged forty at the time of her deaconing. She had been working in Central Africa as a schoolteacher under the auspices of an Anglican missionary organization. Her work in the church overseas led her to accept that her vocation was to an ordained ministry. Linda's local African bishop was very supportive of her but would not ordain a White expatriate as his first female ordinand. He also felt that if she returned to the UK, then she could study at a post-graduate level and protect her future and pension by working for a year or two in a parish in the UK before returning to work in her Central African diocese. This left Linda with two immediate problems: how to gain sponsorship through the selection process; and how to obtain a one-year title parish in the UK before returning to Africa. The first was easily solved in that her father was a priest in the Church of England, and he made the initial contacts for her. The process went smoothly and quickly so that within a few months she was installed at an English theological college and pursuing a post-graduate diploma in theology at the nearby university.

College was not a particularly positive nor enriching experience. Linda was very culture shocked. Her parents and siblings experienced many illnesses and other traumas during the time of her training. She felt alienated and false-footed. When the time came to search for a training parish, she found that it was not easy. Her sponsoring diocese only had one vacancy. Linda was turned down by another because she was divorced, although she had no intention at that time of remarrying. She had had no children by the marriage, so there was no complication there.

It was by intervention outside the college that a title parish was found for her in a Midlands diocese. There was an unexpected place in an outer-fringe council housing estate of considerable notoriety. The incumbent was not someone that she felt immediately drawn to. Indeed, he seemed almost hostile. Still, it was only a year, since the official plan was still to return to Africa. She also felt that she really had no choice. This offer was made during the Holy Week of her final year at theological college, so time was very short.

About the mooted return to Africa, increasingly she felt that this was morally and spiritually questionable. What right had Linda to be a role model for women of another culture? What right had Linda to be alongside another church's struggle when her own faced turmoil over the issue of the ordination of women to the priesthood? And all the time there was that sense of alienation, the constant polite remarks about her speed of entry to training and about the unusual pattern that was mooted for her future. The insularity of the Church of England seemed suffocating, she recalls.

Not being a natural celibate, Linda had invested some time during college in working out her theology about the remarriage of divorced people. This proved to be of personal use since at her deaconing she met someone to whom she felt very drawn. It would take something as cataclysmic as ordination to make Linda accept God was calling her to remarriage. Her new-found love was me, a curate in a nearby parish. I was eight years younger than Linda, unmarried, and Black, British-born to a Black African father by descent and a White English mother.

I was thirty-two at the time of my deaconing. I had felt a vocation to the ordained ministry as a very young man, always having been involved in church life. I received no encouragement for a number of years, rather the reverse. I obtained a degree in sociology and became a social worker and trade union activist. The nagging of the call to priests' order continued, and this time I was accepted and went into one of the older and more prestigious colleges to do my training. I obtained with comparative ease a title post in Coventry Diocese, which had sponsored me.

Linda and I were an item, which seems to have made a radical change to the way in which various diocesan officers treated us. Their attitude changed from one of bonhomie to a more suspicious stance. I was given erroneous and potentially damaging advice about when to seek a move and was offered very little support by the diocese. So, our courtship proceeded, as had the ordination process, with considerable expedition. The added complication was Linda's divorced status. At the time it was still illegal for someone to seek Holy Orders while married to, or intending to marry, someone whose previous spouse was still alive. How crazy was that?

We consulted our bishop, who gave us his blessing but warned us to stay out of the newspapers. The new bill that would permit such marriages had not then been promulgated and an appeal was pending. Parliament had made its mind clear, but there were still some legalities to be clarified. If news of the engagement became public, and if someone complained to the bishop, then he would be forced to suspend his intention to priest me. So, either I could renounce my fiancée and proceed to priesthood, or I could renounce priesthood and remain a deacon alongside Linda. Either way, the relationship would be in jeopardy of serious impairment. So, what was the Church and nation doing putting people in such a position?

Linda's training vicar seemed ambivalent about the relationship. He professed himself astonished at the speed with which we as a couple had come to a common mind even though the many hours of discussion and prayer were explained to him. It seemed humiliating that grown people should be subjected to such scrutiny, but we tried to bear it with good grace. My training vicar seemed completely dismayed by the new relationship and offered merely tepid support.

Meanwhile we had an impact on the Continuing Ministerial Education group that would have suggested to an outsider reading the reports that our behavior was outrageous. We were accused of unsettling the group because of "the strength of our presence." Once our connection was understood, the attitude of the group leaders underwent considerable adjustment. There were smutty comments about Linda's legs and whether she was wearing stockings from one male leader to which she gave a fairly robust response, which silenced any further comment, but it signaled the start of a highly sexualized response to us as a couple, which we located within the racism of the leaders. The classic combination of large Black man and small White woman still raised conflicting emotions and responses in the very White group. Reports amounting to character assassination were made on us. If we had been in secular employment, then our trades union representatives would have had a field day on our behalf.

Linda's training vicar announced that Linda would be welcome to remain in her post as his curate but only if she lived in the parish. Since I did not drive this was not practicable. My house was five minutes away by car, so Linda drove, but this was not agreeable to her vicar. During her time as a curate there, Linda lost count of the number of times that her house was broken into. The place was violent, dangerous, and deeply racist, as comments on the street evinced when we walked around together. A few months later, the incumbent was taken ill and was obliged to leave the parish, due in large measure to the strain of living there. Before he went, he effectively ended Linda's stipendiary ministry by neglecting to send in her first-year report and by taking no action in her support whatsoever. He seemed surprised that he might even have been expected to act on her behalf.

The financial position of the Church of England had become very serious. The commissioners had lost vast sums of money. The dioceses were looking for every possibility to reduce staff. At one time, a job for Linda would have been forthcoming, but now the bishop was forcefully reminded, in front of Linda herself by the diocesan director of ordinands, that a policy had been agreed to pay the post, not the person. With no letter of dismissal or severance, her stipend ceased, and she was obliged to return to teaching.

What annoyed Linda and me was the casual way in which it was assumed that this was no problem, she could always work with me and share my enormous stipend. It was as if Linda was not a real person in her own right, as if she had not successfully pursued a career for two decades and worked in two continents in positions of responsibility. It was also taken for granted that she would soon be having children, despite her age. It seems that it is to be taken as a compliment to have the score of your years reduced by a decade if you are female. Do such a thing to a man and the resulting insult would be clear to everyone.

There was some evidence that one of the diocesan officers deliberately blocked one application that Linda made to a curacy in an inner-city parish. The vicar there was told that he was not to consider her although it would have seemed an ideal place for Linda and her abilities. Certainly, some reports on her made remarks about her character that were less than complimentary. One paper referred to by a senior member of the diocese alleged that the woman was known for being "economical with the truth," which was libelously unfounded.

So, Linda was in secular employment, married to me, with no formal connection with the Church at all. She could hardly attend the parish church where I worked, not least because her ecclesiology did not permit her to sit in the congregation as a lay person, not to mention the formal views of that parish, who were collectively opposed to the ordination of women to the priesthood. She bore with thin fortitude the many remarks made in jest by members of the public asking what on earth she could have done to be sacked, since all manner of criminals and deviants were known to have been retained in stipendiary ministry.

Linda approached the rural dean to let him know that she was available for cover in the area. He suggested that she work in his parishes. She again did not feel particularly drawn to the man. They shared very little; their intellectual and church traditions were very different. But she felt she had no choice. During this time Linda was frequently ill. She kept having bouts of flu that were slow to go. She was diagnosed as asthmatic and started daily treatment. There was continued concern about a lump in a breast. She was also diagnosed as suffering from chronic fatigue syndrome. Her GP suggested that she give up work for a year, but she was keenly aware that if she did that, at her age, then she might never work again, so she struggled on. By now, she was in her second temporary teaching job as I was looking for my own parish, which made her reluctant to accept a permanent job knowing that we might move within months. Earlier we had both been advised by our diocese that we should approach the archbishop's advisor on appointments to seek a joint move. The advisor was apparently surprised at this advice and urged us that I, at least, should complete my title parish in the usual way. However, I came under some pressure from my training incumbent, who informed me that there was a time limit on my curacy. It became a matter of some urgency to secure another post. As it turned out the next assistant curate at St. Mary's Abbey, Nuneaton, caused this vicar considerable trouble, and I cannot but help think it served him right.

So, while I was scouring the country for a parish, Linda continued with the unsatisfactory rural dean. He paid such little attention to what she said that when she asked for his prayers before an operation to remove the lump from her breast, he later claimed that he did not know that she was undergoing an operation at all. He would order her to spend time doing various activities as if she were not a volunteer. The diocese also seemed to take this attitude, expecting her to attend meetings during the daytime when she was at work. Her explanations for non-attendance or for lateness were always met with barely concealed incredulity.

Then, on Ash Wednesday, the rural dean was due to discuss rotas for Lent and Easter. He arrived, looked stressed, said, "This is the parting of the ways. Don't come near my parish again," and left, having spent less than five minutes in her company. In considerable shock and distress, Linda contacted several diocesan officials. A meeting was arranged between the two under the aegis of the diocesan officer for women's ministry. The rural dean said that he did not understand what was going on. He later withdrew from any further meeting. It was left to the diocesan officer for women's ministry to proclaim that the moral high ground was with Linda and that the diocese had treated her badly and basically abandoned her because she had obeyed what she thought was God's will and had stayed in this country and had married. Linda still maintains that if she had married a nice, safe, White priest, then her life would have been much more serene so far as the Church was concerned.

When the time came for me to look for a first solo parish, I found that the circumstances in the Church had changed fundamentally from the outlook predicted in my college days. Posts were scarce and competition fierce. During my curacy I gained a master's degree, which made me a suitable candidate for chaplaincy posts in academic institutions. I was not shortlisted on applications and again, usually, would discover that the person appointed had fewer academic qualifications than I did and had less experience of academic life. For a while it looked as if I would have to accept another curacy, which I was loathed to do. Then out of the blue I received an invitation from Bradford Diocese to look at a post in Little Horton. Accepting this post was a big mistake. My story can be found in my first book, *Mission, Anguish and Defiance*.[2] I remain alert to any possibility of dissension and am sensitive to any sign of tension. I continued with my research, which has been my salvation and sanity.

Once again, Linda managed to pick up a temporary job in teaching while looking for something more permanent. She still had hopes that a stipendiary post might be forthcoming. She was doing quite a bit of cover in a neighboring parish to mine that was in an interregnum. It seemed ideally convenient, so she made a formal application to be considered for the post of priest-in-charge. The archdeacon wrote back saying that he could not consider her a serious candidate. This was a man who had sat in our own drawing

2. Isiorho, *Mission, Anguish and Defiance*.

room and had asked Linda if she had "a little job" (his exact words!) and if she could drive to get there each day. What a stupid, misogynistic, and spiteful man we had to deal with.

With the stipendiary avenue thus exhausted Linda set about job-hunting yet again. She obtained a temporary post as year head in a middle school, later moving to language development teaching. This was precarious at the best of times, due to the vagaries of Home Office funding. At one point, neither Linda nor I had any immediate certainty of employment since I, too, was experiencing severe difficulties with the Church. Linda was shortlisted for a job as a head of department in a large local secondary school but had to withdraw because of the uncertainty of my position, and we were living in a house provided by the church. I did obtain a post back in the Midlands and Linda secured yet another temporary job there while looking for something permanent. By now she was forty-six.

At last Linda had a middle management post in a secondary school, having worked in nine schools over the last six years, and was licensed as a non-stipendiary minister to a nearby parish. She continues to be vexed that the people respond warmly to her while the hierarchy of the Church seems to regard her as a non- or half-person. Linda does not regret that she gave up a very pleasant, fulfilling, and comfortable life overseas but remains puzzled as to why she is not welcome in the Church here, so far as the seniors are concerned, despite the oft publicized and bewailed shortage of priests. Linda rejects the character assessments that have been made of her as a species of rather sad projections. This seriously impairs the openness that was once the hallmark of how Linda likes to do mission. However, Linda is thankful that she shares some of God's sense of humor, without which she could well have lost all sense of her vocation.

. . . .

Another Story

Our second case study in global majority heritage focuses on a Black male priest of Nigerian origin speaking English as a second language. He has been working in these islands for many years. He is married to a White English woman. They have three adopted children who are of mixed race. This is a man of passionate commitment to the gospel and to the notions of justice and freedom under the merciful eye of God. The context is hospital chaplaincy, and his pastoral skills are beyond question when he is observed working either with staff or patients or with families and friends, as I can confirm from personal observation. Our subject has had a succession of jobs within the Church of England. It is easier to gain sector ministry work than to remain in the mainstream, as many who are perceived as belonging to outgroups will testify. Such is the context with the priest in our second case study, who has sought to use the gifts of suffering that have been sent to him to enrich and deepen his ministry to others.

Over the years, our case study has made his views on the injustice of his treatment at the hands of the Church a matter for the courts of law. This has given him a reputation for being litigious and difficult. It is alleged that he is temperamentally unstable and over-emotional. As with the previous case study, he is of academic turn and uses his intellectual gifts to analyze his situation. He has a master's degree. This was not held as a credit but rather as a marker of suspicion against him. This concurs with Linda's experience having been informed by a senior churchman that she was too clever for own good.

Recently our subject has had a mention in several national newspapers because he won an award in an industrial tribunal against a certain hospital trust that discriminated against him during the selection process for a vacancy. He argued that he met all the stated criteria but was not accorded equal status during the recruitment process. Since our subject is in sector ministry and not entirely under the Church's authority, there are nationally recognized guidelines for recruitment, unlike the ad hoc adumbrations of the Church's selection processes.

The hearing upheld his case and costs were awarded to the value of several thousand pounds, signally a significant victory for rationality and justice. As always, the burden for the oppressed in fighting for equity falls upon our own shoulders, and our subject, and his family, have had to endure much loneliness and strain and financial cost over the years.

The last post that our research participant held in this country drove him almost to breaking point with a combination of unheeding management, huge changes in the structures of management of the NHS, and clergy colleagues colluding behind his back to ensure that he was not left in a position of seniority. Black people usually find that a White person is, officially or unofficially, seen as their minder. It will come as no surprise that the part-time assistant chaplain was a White man who set out to undermine our subject's authority. Our subject was well able to argue his case and to present documentation that was carefully and rigorously constructed. His concerns were to establish modern practice in the chaplaincy provision within the Trust that he was working for, including ecumenical and multi-faith aspects.

The documentation that our subject presented was not dealt with readily. There were long delays. At some point our subject was taken ill due, in part, to what he refers to as "my massive bereavement" when he lost several very close family members in circumstances that were deeply distressing. I wish to note at this point that there have been instances of White priests suffering less trauma, in terms of numbers of loss, who have been given leave of absence for extended periods of up to a year and who have been offered sensitive and sympathetic support. This is wonderful, naturally, and to be commended in any bishop that such care is offered to those in stipendiary ministry, but it is also to be noted that a species of blame was attached to our subject as if he were not to be a human being who could be grief-stricken.

During this time, the assistant chaplain also submitted a development plan to the Trust which directly opposed that of his senior in several significant respects. The issue centered on how a further full-time post should be created and filled. Our subject argued that since this was clearly going to be a new post then it should be advertised nationally in accordance with guidelines. If it were advertised merely locally or in-house, then there would not be a field of candidates that would secure a sound appointment. The volume of patients and their declared religious adherence suggested that a full-time Nonconformist minister was not so much needed as an Anglican. Our subject would therefore be clearly in charge of another subordinate, who might be a White male. And this seemed to present something of a stumbling block. If a White female could have been guaranteed, then maybe all would be well. Unknown to our subject, a White woman was gently canvassed; later a Black male was similarly approached. I had knowledge and insight here that the powers that be would rather I did not have.

Papers provided by our subject indicate that there was a distinct personal edge in proceedings that he did not feel originated with him. He explained that he found that his views were being marginalized and that his substantiated arguments were being dismissed as rooted in personal animosity. He stresses that this makes him angry because it is untrue of him. Interestingly, one of his major arguments was for the provision of the spiritual needs of faiths other than Christianity. So here we have an intelligent Black male presenting the case for the rights of other Black people, who in this context are not Christian; this is in a city where a significant proportion of the population are adherents of faiths other than Christianity. Their needs had not been identified as any kind of issue before the actions of our subject.

The assistant chaplain resisted attempts to set up a clear system for feedback to the chaplain. In a busy hospital stretched over three large sites in a sprawling city, procedures for formal feedback were essential. A three-month study leave pushed the two further out of touch. The assistant produced notice boards, without any consultation, that were specifically Christian in relation to the chaplaincy. This directly contravened the Patients' Charter. The assistant also felt that it was ethical and professional to consult with other part-time chaplains and with managers without reference to the chaplain, without even informing him. The resulting confusion made the simplest task fraught with hazards.

Our subject told me that his line manager appeared embarrassed by his expression of his anger at the cavalier way in which the chaplaincy planning was being handled. Without warning, one morning he was summoned to a meeting that afternoon with a hospital manager and the acting bishop. There was no agenda presented for this meeting, but it became clear that our subject was to be ordered to rest because his judgment was "impaired," and his mental state was in question. It is stunning to note that the acting bishop offered what he deemed support by explaining that he had lived in South America and understood that such people became irrational when angry. Since our subject had no connection with this huge section of the globe, he could only conclude that a species of virulent racialization was at work here.

Our subject decided that he would begin the process of finding new employment. He could expect from his experience and from his level of learning and expertise that a large hospital could well see him as a preferred candidate. He found that this was not the case. Indeed, his previous bishop actually and positively worked against him by refusing to allow him to work within his new diocese. This was a very serious situation indeed since the good standing of a member of the Anglican clergy is a legal matter. Our subject sought redress under law and there were several hearings, which dragged on until a satisfactory outcome was obtained. At the direction of the tribune, a full apology was given by the bishop involved. We do not know if there was a financial settlement.

His new bishop did not offer support of any constructive nature to our subject. It is to be noted during his tenure that this new bishop entered a diocese which had four Black clergy in full-time ministry. Within three years that was reduced to one, with no prospect of active recruitment despite the significant proportion of Black and Asian-origin people residing in his diocese. Eventually our subject obtained a new post. His memories of the years of service in the northern Trust are not happy despite his public efforts to serve the needs of all members of the hospital community regardless of their faith. He continued to feel the sense of alienation that I remarked upon earlier. He writes that it is hard to resist the stereotypical depiction of the English stiff upper lip, but this, in shorthand, is what he works with. Perhaps in some way it reassures his White colleagues that they really can ask him where he came from but, when he makes references to his own first language and the rich heritage of wisdom through the Yoruba tradition, I can affirm that reactions from White colleagues do not betray interested respect. It seems that the best he can hope for is a type of toleration that is perilously close to patronizing, and thus dehumanizing, this most human and kind of pastors.

Case Studies in Global Majority Heritage—Conclusion

The case studies in this chapter are idiographic and qualitative. They deal with a narrative that reveals processes that are clearly to my mind proof of generic racism and, as such, provides us with historical data to support our accumulated argument about English ethnicity which is contemporary and ongoing. The main difficulty that our research participants report is how their treatment at the hands of the institutionalized Church witnesses to their community and circle of acquaintance. They feel that they have been forced into a position of challenge and implicit blame of the Church, which they all regarded as their spiritual home. Those who took part in this study were prepared to raise the question of racism and racialization. However, the hierarchy of the Church of England does not seek to deal with this level of reality, especially when they are very actively involved in the process. It is as if the vitality of sin operating within the human heart and at the center of the institution of the Church cannot be acknowledged by senior officeholders. Yet the crucified and suffering Lord who hangs before us on the cross is all about that reality. Church leaders compromise themselves by their polite inability to see the issues for what they are. It is unlikely that a handful of token and ethnically diverse leaders will fare any better.

Chapter Two

"Race" Related Issues and Their Theology of Context

Introduction

THIS CHAPTER FOCUSES ON Church reports about inner cities and the social enterprise agenda. The urban cities and large towns are where most Black and Asian people live in the UK. It is in this context that people from a global majority heritage are subject to economic and social deprivation. Newspapers are not produced or read in a vacuum but in the economic and political context of their day. This chapter is not a stand-alone essay but rather an attempt to provide a theology of context for the reporting process of the religious press.

    The wider context of the mission-shaped Church agenda can be found in Church reports whose initial focus was social responsibility and evangelism among the urban poor. Increasingly this focus has moved in the direction of social cohesion within and between faith communities which has been related to the economics of well-being. This context is increasingly ecumenical with the Church of England and the Methodist Church working as mission partners. This chapter sets out to review three ecumenical reports: *Faithful Cities*[1]; *Unemployment and the Future of Work*[2]; and *Prosperity with a Purpose*.[3] I relate their findings to the concept of social capital and the theology of well-being. I argue that notions of social capital and faithful capital are too anodyne to effect useful change at the policy level. Furthermore, at a time when peak oil has been reached, our structures are perilously close to collapse. This book is mindful of the fragility of any human institution built upon the rapacity and callousness of capitalism. It is always the most disempowered who suffer the most pressure. In our society the so-called people of color and the asylum seeker live at far margins, and that is the context in which we find them in the pages of *The Church Times* and *The Church of England Newspaper*.

I also engage with the Church of England report *Moral, but No Compass*[4] to ask questions about an enterprise agenda which claims to promote social ownership and cohesion. I have chosen these reports to examine how Church policy has changed over time. Central thinking does not necessarily change praxis at the grassroots level, let alone effect mission-shaped changes.

So, what is the fit between these reports and their predecessor, *Faith in the City*? Is there a shared theology or context into which they can be located? I summarized the achievements of the *Faith in the City* as follows. The report conveyed information concerning the social ills that blight the life of the poor in the inner cities and outer fringes. They make a sorry list: unemployment, poor housing, drugs, and prostitution. The endeavors of the Church and the government are recognized but so too are the difficulties in seeking to meet the needs of the disparate group of urban poor. *Faith in the City* did not focus exclusively on urban priority areas (UPAs), as it reflects on the major issues that face us all in the struggle to improve people's lives. Recommendations

1. Vision and Justice Commission, *Faithful Cities*.
2. Council of Churches for Britain and Ireland, *Unemployment and Future of Work*.
3. Churches Together in Britain and Ireland, *Prosperity with a Purpose*.
4. Davis et al., *Moral, but No Compass*, 13.

were made showing empathy with those with blighted lives and making some comments about the invasiveness of the demands of capital. The dangers of exclusion are highlighted including a suggestion that it would be somehow un-British to leave people to languish on the margins of the mainstream because of blips in the market system. There was no real understanding of the inherent sinfulness of capital.

However, to say that the report locates the problems within those adversely affected would not be fair. It is made clear that there are political processes at work that exclude the powerless by favoring the powerful. The report was also clear that this type of brutal exclusion can also be a process of racism; it does not cover over the urban experiences of racial harassment, violence, and the inequities that can be seen in some policing and judicial procedures. The report notes that the Department of the Environment sees ethnicity as an indicator of deprivation. It also ponders that undeniable fact that the majority of people of color live in the urban environment despite being a minority in the UK as a whole. So "decisive action" was called for to support the urban poor despite the acknowledgment that the Church is not seen as crucial in the daily lives of these people. The report saw the Church as working more at the strategic level than the operational.

However, at the grassroots level, churches were asked to be sensitive to local cultures, including working with other denominations, even including Black majority churches—a sadly immigrant-host model. Meanwhile on the national stage the report did recommend that a Commission for Black Anglican Affairs be established for two main reasons: to challenge disadvantage and discrimination and to nurture Black vocations in the Church of England. We can track the effectiveness of *Faith in the City* by examining in later reports how far it had changed policy and radicalized praxis.

To make sense of *Faithful Cities* and the enterprise agenda as context for mission we need to ask some searching questions about White majority churches in general and the Church of England in particular serving Black communities in large urban areas. The theology of context is key here. The Church of England published a series of essays, *God in the City*, commissioned by the archbishop of Canterbury's Urban Theology Group.[5] I want to look at four of these, starting with Ruth McCurry's "Ten Years On,"[6] which reviews events since *Faith in the City*. She comments:

> Some new wine has been making its way through the veins of the old Church and giving it the courage to face the onslaughts of the press and the reproaches of those who do not want change. And 1,400 new women priests in place of up to 200 departing men has rewarded this courage and started another process as important as that started by Faith in the City.[7]

This sounds grand, but McCurry never actually specifies what this process is, so we are left rather in the dark. The second piece comes from Gill Moody and looks at context and the working out of what faith means through this process, which is more helpful. So, we are left with more questions than answers. For example, is there some marker of success, some rewards to be had, for having women priests, which has a further question as to how far in these women have been permitted to inhabit the Church at every level? Has the Church woken up in a welcoming and empowering way to these women? Is it true that being Black is worse than being poor?

This air of confusion is continued in our second piece by Gill Moody, "Life in the City."[8] She makes this remark about clergy in UPAs:

> Some UPA clergy report a conversion in preaching style, especially in areas with large numbers of Black and Asian residents...[9]

Why should it be a cause of astonishment that moving from one context to another affects the style of preaching? It is

5. Sedgwick, *God in the City*.
6. McCurry, "Ten Years On."
7. McCurry, "Ten Years On," 8.
8. Moody, "Life in the City."
9. Moody, "Life in the City," 11.

a response to context that is a genuine marker of prayerful ministry; it is not directly caused by being in the presence of people of color per se. It would cause surprise however if Moody was writing from the perspective of someone who assumed that there was a White methodology deemed to be correct until a change in thinking in response to a change in context had led to a new view. In short, her comment on preaching is unnecessary. The following makes my point clearer:

> Black Anglicans have a great deal to teach predominantly White congregations about prayerful and enthusiastic styles of worship. The common assumption that Black people have a lot to offer to the Church because they have a good sense of rhythm is patronizing and diverts attention away from the main issues. Where Black people are fully involved in the life of a congregation, that church is more able to pose itself critical questions about how it responds to the gifts among its worshippers. It is able to forge a life for itself which is sensitive to people's culture.[10]

This presents Black people as useful in a perspective that is pragmatic and utilitarian. Surely the argument that Black people have a lot to give is as patronizing as the assumptions about our naturally rhythmic endowments—I speak as a dyspraxia! Do other groups have to justify their existence in the Church of England? That is the Church we are all members of unless we opt out, after all. And what if you have no particular use? No distinct marker of difference? Is the White church, represented here by Moody, becoming aware of the falling numbers of White congregants? Are we to be some kind of literal stopgap?

Moving to our next essay, Margaret Walsh is a sister of the Infant Jesus, living in Heath Town, Wolverhampton. She writes about telling other people's stories from her base in this outer-fringe area of deprivation. Her style comes across as very patronizing as she uses these stories to tell White, middle-class Anglicans that Black people live lives of hardship. She cites various anecdotes and statistics before going on to remark:

10. Moody, "Life in the City," 14.

> *A cabinet minister declaration that there is no poverty in Britain must rank as the most fatuous public statement of the decade.*[11]

She describes life on benefits and the debt trap that so many fall into despite their best efforts. Before she goes on to look at the preferential option for the poor, she makes this comment on Heath Town:

> *In recent months we have seen an increase in the levels of aggression being expressed and experienced. This can too easily be dismissed as racial tension without addressing the underlying causes. The police maintain a discreet presence, especially when it is a question of domestic disputes. However, they can show their determination to maintain law and order by coming in large numbers, armed with riot shields and supported by helicopter and search lights as happened on the night of 23rd May 1989 when we had what have become known as the Heath Town Riots. People have lost confidence in such protection and defend themselves as best they can. We have to expect the occasional violent incident.*[12]

She writes solely from her own perspective in Heath Town and does not make any connections beyond, no look at how police operate generally let alone at the oppression continuing across the Western world as people, objectified by capital, are discarded like dross. With the near collapse of the global economic markets in 2010, writing from my perspective in 2010, we could see a line of oppression and exclusion continuing unabated.

Walsh also says:

> *I see very clearly the values which are most important in Britain today: classroom success, knowing the right people, a competitive spirit, White skin, and an address in leafy suburbia.*[13]

---

11. Walsh, "Here's Hoping," 55.
12. Walsh, "Here's Hoping," 55–56.
13. Walsh, "Here's Hoping," 60.

She does acknowledge that poor connotes Black in much of the Church's dialogue. She is aware of the complex machinations of the political machinery that controls us:

> *We continue to agonize about structural sin and the root causes of injustice, and we wonder if we are making any progress in either understanding or changing the situation. The system is far too complex for us and sometimes we find ourselves standing silent before it, as Jesus did during his trial (John 19).*[14]

This is a fascinating piece of reflection concerning our ability to manage the very structures that we have created. Who is the "us" she refers to? Is she seeing us as victims of our own systems? Or does she see us, Pilate-like, opting out of something rather challenging for sure, but in our remit as humans? "Standing silent before the system" comes across as opting out of our God-given responsibility to be responsible stewards of this creation.

"Distilling the Wisdom," an essay by David Ford and Laurie Green, evaluates the current state of urban theology via a review of the work of their fellow contributors. Ford and Green tell us they:

> *. . . were fascinated at the number of times comments were diametrically opposed to one another, as if to prove our contention that urban theology simply has to be provisional, diverse and fragmentary if it is to do justice to UPA experience.*[15]

What does this mean? These are serious questions, the answers to which can have a great impact on people's lives. If these experts were really doing contextual theology, then they would have come up with some answers, some solutions, at various levels from the strategic to the operational. This should not be couched in the same mode of discourse as a polite seminar somewhere in the academy, fascinating but unearthed. This is the archbishop's board and it ought to have some serious clout, so there is no need for the tentative tone. At the very least, the contributors should have had

---

14. Walsh, "Here's Hoping," 71.
15. Ford and Green, "Distilling the Wisdom," 24.

the time to come out with a united voice giving a common world view. The one commonality appears to be that people who live in urban priority areas are different and different rules should apply to them. Furthermore, Black people who are clearly associated with these areas of deprivation are very different indeed. This reminds me of the senior cleric who remarked to my wife, then working in a UPA parish, that there must be some wonderful people there, to which my wife robustly replied that it was a brutal, ugly place that frequently produced brutal, ugly behavior.

Ken Leech argued many years ago that the Church of England is an organization that can face two ways at the same time.[16] On the one hand, it calls for radical changes in society to combat poverty and racism while, on the other hand, it gives support to a dominant value system that gives rise to inequality. This structured hypocrisy was seen in Church reports about the inner cities because these documents do not recognize the privileged position from which they originate.[17] Furthermore, the Church's own structures reflect and reinforce the system to which Church leaders claim to be in opposition. Without adequate self-criticism, how can the Church maintain anything other than a patronizing presence among the urban poor? Thus, the Church of England according to Leech had engaged in both class and racial discrimination, and its credibility among the working class was almost non-existent.[18] It is certainly true that, historically, Black Anglicans from the Caribbean had taken the place of the White working class until the Black Christians were forced out by existing White congregations. Today the Church of England continues to function as an affluent, White institution within a society divided by class and race.

So how did the Church of England become involved in the inner cities and, by association, with the Black presence in the UK? Leech suggests that we trace this involvement back to the housing issues of the Rachmanism years.[19] At that time, the Church was

16. Leech, *Struggle in Babylon*.
17. Leech, *Struggle in Babylon*, 20.
18. Leech, *Struggle in Babylon*, 23.
19. Leech, *Struggle in Babylon*, 53.

silent. Since then, the Church has developed a conscience about its past financial involvements and the slums that provided accommodation for migrant labor. *Faith in the City*, and now *Faithful Cities*, can be seen as institutionalized conscience solving.

It was not Leech's argument nor mine that the Church should pull out of the inner cities nor that we should in any way devalue the work done by individual Christians and clergy, but, rather, for that work to be effective, the Church must recognize the alienation that exists between itself and these urban populations. Clearly this means making a distinction between the ministry of those who work in the inner city and the institutionalized focus of the Church, embedded as it is in the established order.

Faith in the City and *Faithful Cities* have no salvific content or eschatology. By this I mean there is little understanding of where the Church has been or where it is going, let alone where it is now. If these reports contain any theology at all, then they represent a way of seeing things from the top down and not from the bottom up. Such an approach never asks what the poor can do for the rich or for themselves. Thus, the Church wants to be nice to the poor, and helping them becomes an opportunity for patronizing them as victims of their own squalor.

Faithful Cities Revisited in the Condition of the Urban Poor

The Anglican/Methodist report *Faithful Cities*[20] advocates the replacement of the minimum wage with an undefined living wage as a package toward a redistribution of wealth and as a serious contribution to the debate concerning the economics of happiness in the UK. It also called upon the government of the day to defer the deportation of asylum seekers, allowing them to enter the workplace while decisions were made as to their longer-term future. Combating racism becomes the responsibility of faith communities, and more resources need to be given to youth and community work.

20. Vision and Justice Commission, *Faithful Cities*.

This report was produced by the Commission on Urban Life and Faith and was published jointly by the official publishing arm of the Church of England, Church Publishing and the Methodist Publishing House, in 2005. The commission itself was an ecumenical working party whose purpose was to facilitate discussion and action among those who inhabit the urban context and those who are responsible for policies that directly affect these communities. And like the authors of *Faith in the City* twenty years earlier they wanted to bring to the attention of the government the impact of social policy. Their emphasis now was less on urban destitution and disadvantage than on what constituted a good city following regeneration and its ability to accommodate ethnic and religious pluralism. Clearly, within that context the churches and other faith communities would have to redefine their role considering their concept of neighbor if they were to be agents of change.

The view is often expressed that the churches are maintaining a Christian presence in the cities and in urban areas of deprivation and that this presence can be identified not exclusively as Anglican but certainly English. It is also recognized that Black worshipers had in the past been excluded from these structures through institutionalized racism in the contemporary affairs of church and state. Emphasis has been placed upon the importance of maintaining resources in deprived areas and, for some Christians, this is a way of demonstrating the church's relevance in a modern world. *Faithful Cities*, although an ecumenical report, has an unbalanced focus upon the Church of England and its continuing presence in the inner city. Other denominations are encouraged to work with the Church of England's Urban Fund or similar inner-city projects. A partnership relationship between the faith communities was recommended as the best way of attracting government resources for community development and ministerial training. The Church's activities are described in the language of outreach and mission. Thus, the cities and urban areas of deprivation are not to be abandoned lest the Church of England should lose its credibility there and everywhere else.

Those who work in the inner cities have no difficulty in providing a considerable list of things which they understand the Church was doing in the cities and urban areas of deprivation. These included supported Church schools, attracting grants from other organizations as well as deploying its own resources, maintaining its buildings, maintaining clergy in those areas, looking for new forms and styles of worship, and keeping the mission work of the Church alive for the local communities they were supporting. They usually want more mission and outreach that would include help for the poor and the under-privileged. However, there is a very real danger that resources are being wasted in the cities and urban areas of deprivation. The thrust of this argument is that the churches are engaging in self-congratulatory campaigns which direct community energies into non-threatening and apolitical projects. If this is true, then these mission strategies can only result in the alienation of people from the institution of the Church. So, what can be done? I feel that we should be asking political questions about the distribution of resources, and the Church should try to act as a bridge between the poor and those in positions of authority.

In conversations with White clergy about the inner cities and the Church's role there are usually considerably more references to the Church's mission or outreach than there is to *Faithful Cities* or even its predecessor, *Faith in the City*. People are selective about which aspects of this program they want to see developed, and they make their choices with little consideration of the difficulties that would and should face the Church as a change agent. Their theology does not really go beyond "Let us be kind to the urban poor." However, the language of inner-city projects is a clear justification for the Church's continual presence. Many well-meaning White clergy understand the Church's role to champion the poor by providing resource centers and to engage in a certain amount of community work to gain credibility. This in turn would make the Church accessible to the helpless and, with the introduction of user-friendly liturgy, bring people into Church. There was also a strong feeling that this Christian presence had to be defended rather than defined, a subtle but crucial difference that marks the boundary between making a presence and making a change.

Much is made in *Faithful Cities* about diversity, although there are no tangible suggestions to address the fear and exclusion of racism associated with urban life. We are told that nothing is monochrome, and that sub-cultural diversity now includes sexual politics.[21] To its credit, the report does not equate racial diversity with contact and greater understanding between cultures, as familiarity can just as easily lead to contempt as to acceptance.[22] Racism is recognized as a problem with institutionalized dimensions and that, as a social phenomenon, is unlikely to go away as the result of multicultural education.

Having raised the issue of racial injustice, *Faithful Cities* should have related this to the mechanisms of exclusion within church and society. It is unclear whether the report writers preferred to blame the system rather than the quality of leadership provided by senior office holders. This raises the further question as to who gets to be on these reporting bodies and how they are recruited, through which networks. White Christians, unlike their Black counterparts, do not stress the importance of Black leadership within the Church. White clergy are happy to talk about change as part of their work among the urban poor, but that is often as far as it goes. This means I must ask: How committed are our churches in challenging such injustice? How will they tackle Church structures that perpetuate racialized injustices?

Many White churches are reluctant to use the word *racism* even though they recognize some of its mechanisms. We can only speculate as to why they should hold back from naming it, perhaps the same sort of genteel bowdlerism that characterized some of the more prudish excesses of Victorian England. It certainly reinforces Black exclusion. Can we argue that this group of White Christians were sensitive of their own history as White people in English society in the operation of a policy of exclusion? The natural inclination is not to declare your own culpability, and so

21. See chapter 2 of Vision and Justice Commission, *Faithful Cities*.
22. Vision and Justice Commission, *Faithful Cities*, 20.

the word *racism* is not used. Clearly, people do not always differentiate between collective responsibility and individual guilt, especially where defense mechanisms are in operation.

Unemployment and the Future of Work

Jesus proclaimed in the Gospel of St. Matthew that poor will always be with us.[23] But what did he mean by this? It certainly does not mean indifference to the plight of the poor. To my mind it means we must engage in a constant battle to challenge inequality and disadvantage. It could also mean a realization that the poor do not have the means to change things because they are disadvantaged at many levels including education. Furthermore, many poor people are so disadvantaged that they will participate in the politics of their own impoverishment. The classic example of this is support for politicians who offer tax breaks and the selfish idea of not paying for the welfare of others.

The report implicitly blames unemployment on poor school achievement but does explain that responsible employers should take their share of the task of educating a worker adequately—that's all those good employers out there—but the report does sensibly acknowledge the need for regulation to bring the market economy into line with its ideas and ideals. *Unemployment and the Future of Work* recognizes that human beings have a natural inclination to learn so the education system must be overhauled to achieve a classless and inclusive society. Amid all this, the poor will become poorer, the marginalized more distant from any sense of inclusion or cohesion. That is what happens with capitalism, which is a very powerful system that will protect its own, long, best interests with assiduity. The dream of *Faithful Cities* seems even less achievable without radical policy shifts at governmental and fiscal levels. Of course, there is a role here for the clarion call for justice to be sounded ever more loudly by the Church, but we seem to have lost the jubilee fervor of the millennium. And maybe we

23. Matt 26:11.

will have to accept that not all people will be able to make a gainful and a meaningful living by working, which is one of the central tenets of a church inquiry called *Unemployment and the Future of Work*. This was the product of an ecumenical working party, the Council of Churches for Britain and Ireland, whose intention was to champion the idea of full employment. This report predates *Faithful Cities* but many of the ideas—taxation, public spending, minimum wage, the benefit system—find their way into the latter and are presented as new, innovative ways of looking at market economics and employment issues. Many of the solutions put forward appear contradictory so that the whole report amounts to a collection of policy proposals which could well, so the report says, reduce unemployment and so empower some of the oppressed within British society. The dependence upon public funding for some of these schemes may not be practicable.

There is some encouragement to be had in the fact that *Unemployment and the Future of Work* does question the machinations within state capitalism. It expects the Church to be ready to challenge in this area, but there are none of the fundamental questions that would lead Christians to inquire how state capitalism can ever possibly be consonant with the gospel.

> *Christianity and the market system have never been altogether at ease with one another, and probably never will be. To put it no stronger, the market does not actively encourage the Christian virtues of compassion and generosity; neither does it promote social justice or moderation in the enjoyment of material things. On the contrary it sometimes excuses or even encourages a kind of selfishness and a kind of callousness which would be totally unacceptable if they were shown in relationships face-to-face. It may also be a vehicle for ambition and greed, or an obsessive need to accumulate wealth.*[24]

These queries are offset by the positive aspects offered by the market system, according to this report:

---

24. Council of Churches for Britain and Ireland, *Unemployment and the Future of Work*, 24.

> *Some of these unattractive features of the market system have been very much in evidence, alongside much that is good, in our society over the last twenty years or so.*[25]

There is much laudable talk about good employers wanting to work together with the government to create jobs and therefore wealth for as many people as possible. What the authors do not seem able fully to comprehend is that it is profit for oneself that drives entrepreneurs and other businesspeople. Altruism is not a universally acknowledged virtue. And while, yes, it is true that work can be a creative process and can fit within a Christian work ethic, nevertheless the authors again fail to grasp that for many workers their employment is strictly a means to an end, something to be endured with that quiet desperation. Perhaps the authors are showing their social class in this assumption, a certain ivory-tower optimism? To its credit, however, the report does see that overwork is indicative of unfair practice and it does make a distinction between work and income.

Gender issues do receive some fleeting attention here; apparently it is necessary to inform church people that women are now often involved in paid work, which results in a double burden of work for them as they continue to look after the home and the children. The report does not come to terms with the social process that sees more women entering the workplace as increasing numbers of men leave it or are forced out. The historical record of women's paid work being consistently lower in cash value than men's is not explored nor seen for the gross injustice that it is.

If the central concern of this report is that the labor market should be based upon principles of fairness, then it should give clear direction as to how that laudable goal could be achieved. Christianity bespeaks generosity, compassion, and justice, which certainly puts a tension, if not an outright opposition, between the church and capitalism. Interestingly, the report concludes that modern trade unionism is responsible and forging a new relationship with

---

25. Council of Churches for Britain and Ireland, *Unemployment and the Future of Work*, 24.

the employers. Trade unions are now compatible with Christianity, which is where many of their roots lie after all:

> *There is a long tradition of support for responsible unionism in the churches. The spirit of co-operation has a strong appeal to Christians, provided it is not just the solidarity of one group to improve its own position at the expense of others.*[26]

> *We support the view that employers should be required to negotiate with a union where a majority of the workers concerned wish it. At the same time, we recognize that the form of negotiation adopted should take account of the rights of those workers who are not union members and whose views of interests may be different.*[27]

So, we arrive at a position where *Unemployment and the Future of Work* deplores the undue power of the unions during the 1970s while lamenting their decline in the 1990s. The irony of blaming the unions for poverty and low pay in the 1970s while regretting their lower power base in the 1990s is not lost on this reader:

> *The balance of industrial power, which in the 1970's was tipped in favour of the unions, is now too heavily weighted in the opposite direction. As a result many workers are now employed on a take-it-or-leave-it basis. Too often that is the reality behind the comfortable-sounding phrases about individual negotiations and individual contracts.*[28]

Above all the lack of social cohesion is seen as the end cause of unemployment. What is needed is a return to that nostalgic state of the Dunkirk spirit—apparently forgetful of the massive defeat that Dunkirk represents—so that we can revisit this mythical sense of community:

---

26. Council of Churches for Britain and Ireland, *Unemployment and the Future of Work*, 112.

27. Council of Churches for Britain and Ireland, *Unemployment and the Future of Work*, 133.

28. Council of Churches for Britain and Ireland, *Unemployment and the Future of Work*, 26.

> It is arguable that the underlying reason why full employment could be maintained for two decades after the war was that the shared experience of wartime had produced an unusually strong sense of community. Since then social cohesion has weakened; individuals have become more individualistic and economic relationships have become less personal and more remote.[29]

The English appear to have a particular genius for retrospection, and some of these pictures of the past probably never existed. This does not mean that we cannot find a new cohesion now, one that is worked out through dialogue rather than by impositions delivered from above to below in the hierarchical world of past British life. For this sense that, somehow, things should hang together does echo the kingdom and, with the help of the spiritual and social strength of the church, we can look forward to a greater sense of belonging.

The Church of England has an established and understandable mode of discourse so that to hear it using the language of economics, interest rates, budgetary policies does not land well. Sometimes the report argues one way—modifying the National Insurance system, perhaps even dropping it in some cases—while in other places it supports the National Insurance scheme. Having toyed with economics, the report then turns to a grey area termed *the third sector*. In this place, generous employers would be welcoming partners for the Church and would join in, using some public money and some private philanthropy, to generate a creative workplace. To its credit, *Unemployment and the Future of Work* does make it plain that there should be a decent living minimum wage, depicting pay, rightly, as offensive to human dignity. The report speaks out against the huge rewards available in the private sector.

With respect to racial discrimination, *Unemployment and the Future of Work* sees that this has become more entrenched in the workplace in the recent past:

---

29. Council of Churches for Britain and Ireland, *Unemployment and the Future of Work*, 51.

> It is associated with racism, an ideology fundamentally inconsistent with Christian belief. Racial justice depends on access to employment. Nothing will change for people from the Black and ethnic minority communities until they have an economic stake in society.[30]

The authors rely here on the work of the Churches' Commission for Racial Justice (CCRJ). To learn more about this important aspect of their inquiry the authors held a meeting with members of the Churches' Commission for Racial Justice.[31]

> Members of the CCRJ said that the market does not work fairly for people from ethnic minorities. Young Blacks ask what is the point of education when many Black people have achieved educational qualifications and still have no jobs. They need to believe that there is something in society to which they can aspire. . . . Members of CCRJ drew our attention to the legislation against religious discrimination in Northern Ireland as a possible model for tougher laws against racial, as well as religious, discrimination in the United Kingdom as whole.[32]

Unemployment and the Future of Work wanted to see clear monitoring to ensure Black representation at all levels. It takes on board the Sheppard/Wood principles endorsed by the CCRJ.

> These principles were drawn up by Race Equality in Employment, a project of the Ecumenical Committee for Corporate Responsibility. They are a model for positive action to give people from ethnic minorities fair and effective access to work and not positive discrimination which would be against the law. In brief companies should:
>
> 1. adopt a detailed Equal Opportunity Policy;

---

30. Council of Churches for Britain and Ireland, *Unemployment and the Future of Work*, 118.

31. Council of Churches for Britain and Ireland, *Unemployment and the Future of Work*, 116.

32. Council of Churches for Britain and Ireland, *Unemployment and the Future of Work*, 118.

2. *declare an intention to increase employment of Black and minority ethnic workers where they are under-represented;*
3. *undertake positive action to offset any imbalance;*
4. *monitor the ethnic composition of the work force regularly;*
5. *use fair recruitment and selection procedures;*
6. *provide training for employees and potential recruits;*
7. *where equal opportunities are not fully in place, designate an Equal Opportunities Manager;*
8. *make racial and religious harassment serious disciplinary offences;*
9. *publish an annual employee profile with the Annual Report;*
10. *seek actively for a professionally qualified minority ethnic board member.*[33]

The problem here is that the report is placing so much confidence in the notion that employers want to address issues of justice for all, that they truly want to break down the barriers that divide.

With its foray into the realms of the market and economics, the authors of the report wrestle with the social and political phenomenon of the issues around exclusion. What they do not do is to come up with a clear theological interpretation and insight that would allow them to be able to encounter the varying strategies of governments in a meaningful way that would effect change. The authors dodge around the simple truth that market economies and the higher principles of Christianity are not coterminous. To predicate suggestions for the future upon the assumption that all employers would put Christian principles before the profit motive is to doom oneself to failure as a credible and achievement alternative.

---

33. Council of Churches for Britain and Ireland, *Unemployment and the Future of Work*, 116–17.

The Theology of Capitalist Wealth

Continuing the theme of work as rescue, another report, *Prosperity with a Purpose*, also sees solutions to exclusion in the system of state capital. The context of this report is to be found in its appeal to merchant bankers and entrepreneurs. It is a publication of Churches Together in Britain and Ireland and is contemporary with *Faithful Cities*, which borrows heavily from its findings without having to rehearse ethical arguments about affluence. *Prosperity with a Purpose* wants to promote capitalism and trickle-down economics as a preferential option for the poor. The argument is that the poor will be better off in a more prosperous society and may even become affluent themselves as they take moral ownership of the present economic system.

At no time in *Prosperity with a Purpose* are models other than capitalism even tentatively explored, despite biblical possibilities here. Productivity is seen as a driver of increased employment because it engenders economic growth. Paid work is virtuous; living off benefits is not. The government's job is to make people see that. The introduction, therefore, of the job-seeker allowance is seen as benign. This is hardly the view on the street. The fact that women seeking to raise children also are subject to the job seeker allowance and to inducements to return to paid work is good. There is, again, no consideration of other models of community and of child raising. Here we are dealing with social engineering, but the authors of the report seem mildly aware of that, merely urging the government of the day to go beyond a narrow focus on employment issues.

I should explain here in all fairness that *Prosperity with a Purpose* does see connections between social justice and economics, but it cannot see the causal root between one person's wealth and another's impoverishment. The authors seem to believe that the generation of wealth is not an inherently excluding process. Taxation is seen as a method of leveling the playing fields. Risk takers who succeed in acquiring riches play their part through taxation. The creative urge is seen as a driver as much as the desire for profit, which conveys some moral probity to these entrepreneurs who are seen almost as a special class of capital developers. Profit, mammon, is not a term of disapprobation, and Christians should embrace with gusto the market system. The report identifies a virtuous circle of productivity with higher returns for those workers who will engage with ardor and to increase their personal skills base.

Of course, no human system is perfect, that is a given, and this is certainly true of the market economy with the possible developments of political bias and corruption leading to weak controls over monopolies. Competition is seen as a control factor in this Adam Smith worldview. Some threats to this delicate balance are identified such as the collusion of senior managers across organizations to drive up their respective salaries or the problem of too rapacious a system of taxation when the support of good causes can kill the goose that lays the golden egg. In the 2010s, to suggest that enterprise must be rewarded is to rouse the person in the street to decry the huge bonuses paid to merchant bankers. *Prosperity with a Purpose* also recognizes that government can be too fast to react to the rising cost of public services by treating the providers as profit driven rather than service organizations. This has merely and so obviously resulted in a diminution of provision that impacts most severely upon those already at the margins of the prosperous society.

Social Capital and the Enterprise Agenda

Faithful Cities understands the combination of church, voluntary labor, and private enterprise as *social capital*.[34] It is about networking and relationship of economic well-being within a definite market system. It uses the language of human resource management and rational decision-making. Social capital is also known as *faith capital* as it is able to promote cohesion in civil society by equipping it adherents with the skill necessary to make

---

34. Vision and Justice Commission, *Faithful Cities*, 3.

choices between economic strategies that are likely to be for the altruistic common good. Organized religion is encouraged to engage with the private sector for the mutual benefit of both without damaging its charitable status.

Faithful Cities takes on the social capital model of bonding, bridging, and linking as a method of establishing connections between people to form community.[35] Thus, social capital brings together close-knit groups of people working from an already formed structure as well as making connections between groups that are not coterminous. Furthermore, social capital claims to cut across status and boundaries to exert influence through these linking strategies. Relationship of bond with family and friends are described as horizontal while those connected with local and central government are vertical. Thus, faith communities with their traditional core values can mediate between these two dimensions, giving direction to community cohesion that draws upon volunteer labor. Faithful capital is faithful service, which has been exploited for the market system. Thus, the cash value of commitment is found in voluntary labor that does not have to be paid for.

In the Church report *Moral, but No Compass* we are told that the relationship between UK churches and their input to social welfare issues has had a significant impact in a wider debate about English identity politics.[36] However, this same report is also of the opinion that UK faith-based organizations are ill equipped to take on public service contracting, as this is likely to result in unhealthy competition between organizations.[37] The view is expressed here that too great an emphasis has been placed by government upon minority faiths while neglecting the Christian churches who clearly have a strong pull with the indigenous population.[38] We are told that government plans are impractical because they lack a nuanced understanding of what faith groups can offer in terms

---

35. Gilchrist, *Well-Connected Community*.
36. Davis et al., *Moral, but No Compass*, 13.
37. Davis et al., *Moral, but No Compass*, 18.
38. Davis et al., *Moral, but No Compass*, 50.

of social capital.[39] It is claimed that the bridging process of the social capital model would fail because skills and resources between groups are disproportionate. Thus, the mainstream churches would be disempowered and the other faith groups overstretched by the demands of welfare reform. Clearly, *Moral, but No Compass* does not see the churches as one of the many faith groups in the UK but rather as the major third sector player par excellence. And, having made that distinction, it proceeds to talk about minority faiths as the poor relation and to complain about the government's handling of churches. Right wing political groups have for many years expressed similar views about the exclusion of the Christian religion. So, who has lost the compass, if not the plot? Is it the government of the day under New Labour or the Von Hugel Institute commissioned by the Church of England to give direction to its relationship with the welfare state?

So, what about the enterprise agenda; where does it fit in all this? The enterprise agenda amounts to strategic policy initiatives that claim to be beneficial particularly to Black and Asian communities through various programs of urban regeneration. In short, a social enterprise is a capitalistic business, which happens to have some social objectives that can act as its main selling point, a type of local state capitalism in which profits can be reinvested back into the business and vicariously given to the community. Social enterprises bring people together and make them into a community that sees economic development and social gain as synonymous even though the two are claimed to be mutually exclusive. Having said that, and with the benefit, always, of hindsight, it is easy to see how New Labour got very comfortable during its long tenure, particularly under Tony Blair, drawing upon the language of the marketplace as if there were some intrinsic worth to be found there.

Social enterprise takes many forms. Firstly, there are employee-owned businesses whose function could be job creation as part of a regeneration package. Secondly, there are credit unions, which do a valuable job in providing finance to people who could easily find themselves the victims of loan sharks. There are also

39. Davis et al., *Moral, but No Compass*, 20.

cooperatives or associations of like-minded people who jointly own the enterprise, having come together for mutual social and economic reasons. Thirdly there are development trusts sponsored by local authority and their business partners. Fourthly, social firms provide access to employment for disabled and marginalized groups. Fifthly, there are community businesses that have control over local markets.

The notion of a social enterprise comes with an assumption about social aims and social ownership. Social aims can range from job creation and skills training to ethical trading projects. Profits are usually shared between stakeholders who are empowered to form autonomous organizations but are accountable to this structure and the wider community. In its favor social enterprise promotes comprehensive evaluation processes. Thus, social enterprise can be classified as a *third sector* in the production of goods and services. It relies on the public sector and on voluntary charity and, most importantly, on the entrepreneurial skills of private business. However, this form of organization is not different from business because of its partnership with business. They share operational systems, commercial accountability, and legal structures. Management structures of both social enterprise and commercial business are team oriented with an emphasis on the marketing of goods and services. The function of a social enterprise is to provide a surplus as the result of trading.

So does the enterprise agenda dependent upon social capital sit comfortably with a contextual and liberation theology dependent upon a preferential option for the poor? The answer must be no. Social enterprises have access to public funding and it is this that makes them a very attractive partner for private enterprise. As for theology, *Faithful Cities* believes it is following Black theologians in bringing about a synthesis of liberation theologies and Black expressive cultures.[40] If this is how to democratize theology as a practical tool for transformation then the dividing line between commercial exploitation and community participation becomes very thin indeed.

40. Vision and Justice Commission, *Faithful Cities*, para. 2.63.

Conclusion

Despite theoretical arguments to the contrary (and there are many of these in the church reports reviewed in this chapter), to practice Christianity some Christians have found it necessary to reject capitalism. Is there not a basic contradiction between this economic system and Christian belief? Does capitalist wealth find a place in the values of the kingdom? I am fed the old tale, change the individual and then wider circumstances will also change, but my theological sense tells me that this fails to take account of institutionalized misery. Such inner changes minus the wider structural change are idealistic nonsense. Humanity participates in God's creation firstly by using its labor to perfect it—how can we accomplish this in a capitalist society when our labor is not our own and we are compelled to sell it to capital? Surely, a socialist economic system is essential if we are to express our basic Christianity, thus making a reality of a classless society as understood by the Acts of the Apostles.[41]

To take politics out of Christianity is a denial of the truth. It removes faith from reality and assumes that it is a product of the mind, which amounts to a refusal to accept that Christianity is revealed historically and subsequently understood and practiced in an historical context. The history of Christianity is a history of Christian involvement in political order. The Bible reveals God as a political God who acts in history. Jesus refers to the kingdom as community and this surely means a politically structured society on this earth. We must always transfer the teaching of Christ to our own historical situation. This is not to deny that Christ was political in his own day and that, in any conflict between rich and poor, God takes sides with the poor and this is true of all historical periods. To understand the political nature of Christ we need to realize that the political relationship of his time was between the Sadducees and the Romans. Jesus upset that balance and died as a result. So, the death of Jesus had political causes and political consequences. The Bible is crowded with socio-political images,

---

41. Acts 2:44–5 and 4:32.

for example of Jesus identifying himself with human needs, material as well as spiritual. Even when he could be considered apolitical, his message was subversive of all established order. His reply on the question of paying taxes to Caesar reveals this: "give to Caesar what is Caesar's and to God what is God's" (Mark 12:17). If the advice had been followed, the empire would have collapsed, for it was built upon slavery. To give to God what was God's would have meant returning the slaves to him in a state of freedom. Caesar would have been left holding a worthless coin. The exchange of money in the temple in Luke 20 could also be considered a subversive act if it is remembered that the money changing hands was the fruit of Roman exploitation. Christ was a redeemer and liberator, so practical Christianity can only function if is working toward the liberation of humankind. The poor inherit the kingdom of justice and peace, but these are not merely spiritual values but political ones, which need to be given historical form. God does not love from beyond but gives expression to his presence by loving us through each other. He speaks to our social and historical existence. The kingdom has many sides. It is a historical past, present, and future. It is also a social revolution where complete morality is collective and individual. Thus, God is expressed through the community sharing a common ownership for the benefit of all. The mode of production needs to be a caring mode of common use replacing a capitalist, uncaring mode for the profitable few. There is no evidence for Christians ever have been told to ignore the present misery. Our duty is to make this earth a fit and holy place in which to live.

Chapter Three

"Race," Ethnicity, and Black Theology

Introduction

My research into the racialization process and the religious press of the Church of England takes as its starting point previous studies about "race," ethnicity, and membership of a church. The first part of this chapter offers a brief historical review of that research. The second and substantial part of this chapter concentrates upon Black political activism. My argument is that Black theology in the British context owes a great deal to the secular political activism of the late 1960s, culminating in the popular uprisings of the 1980s and 1990s otherwise known as civil disturbances or riots. The chapter concludes with some of the issues arising out of the Church of England report *From Lament to Action*.[1]

---

1. Archbishop's Anti-Racist Taskforce, *From Lament to Action*.

Racial Prejudice and Church Membership

An important starting point in my understanding of the way global majority heritage people are portrayed in *The Church Times* and *The Church of England Newspaper* can be found in the relationship between racial prejudice and Church membership. A re-thinking of Anglicanism and its relationship to the religious press of the Church of England in the mode of involvement of Black and Asian Christians must seek to clarify the pattern of attitudes that convey racial prejudice and racism. So, what is the relationship between racial prejudice and Church membership? The significance of organized religion and religious affiliations for the formation and expression of in-group and out-group sentiments has an established presence in academic literature. Most studies looking into the area of religious and racial prejudice have been conducted in the United States of America. US surveys suggest that churchgoers are likely to be more racially prejudiced than non-churchgoers. Thus, religiosity and racial prejudice were correlated. A high level of religiosity meant a corresponding high level of racial prejudice.[2] However, researchers differentiate between *intrinsic* and *committed* Christians.[3] Those who attend church regularly out of conviction, rather than from a sense of propriety, are no more prejudiced than those who do not attend church. Interestingly, it is the conventional observers of duty who are more prejudiced than either of the other two groups.

Clearly religiosity is identification with a religion and a committed expression of that identification, as in church attendance, indicates a significantly different social correlation. Researchers distinguish between the communal and associational aspects of religious groups. It is a distinction between the commitment of individuals to a socio-religious group, on the one hand, and a commitment to a type of religious orientation that transcends socio-religious group membership, on the other. Associational membership is defined by the frequency of attendance at worship,

---

2. Allport and Kramer, "Some Roots of Prejudice."
3. Allport and Ross, "Personal Religious Orientation."

while communal membership is about the degree of primary relationships that are limited to a particular group. Thus, the groups become those who are actively involved in associational activities and whose involvement with associational groups can be described as marginal. A further classification of religious orientation concerned "doctrinal orthodoxy" and that of "devotionalism."

According to Lenski doctrinal orthodoxy is "that orientation which stresses intellectual assent to prescribed doctrines," while devotionalism is "that orientation which emphasizes the importance of private, or personal communion with God."[4] These religious sub-communities "foster and encourage a provincial and authoritarian view of the world."[5] It is the communal group membership rather than the associational that are linked with racial prejudice. In other words, it is the sub-communities, not the churches, that can be described as intolerant and narrow-minded. The Lenski research considers the differing perceptions that socio-religious groups had of each other in the metropolitan community of Detroit. Religion and racial origin define the boundaries of group membership. The four socio-religious groups include White Protestant; White Catholic; Jew; and Black Protestant.

WHITE PROTESTANT: This group held negative images of all other groups. However, they are perceived favorably by those they criticize.

> Catholics have a more favorable image of Protestants than of Jews, and Jews have a more favorable image of Protestants than of Catholics. On each of three criteria (religious tolerance, business fairness, and power), at least 60 per cent of both Catholics and Jews expressed approval of white Protestants.[6]

In their criticisms of Catholics and Jews, White Protestants employ selective characteristics upon which they construct a negative image.

---

4. Lenski, *Religious Factor*, 25.
5. Lenski, *Religious Factor*, 328.
6. Lenski, *Religious Factor*, 63.

> They are twice as likely to criticize Jews for unfairness in business practices as for religious intolerance . . . . In the case of Catholics, the situation is exactly reversed. They are criticized often for religious intolerance, but seldom for unfair business practices.[7]

WHITE CATHOLIC: This group is less critical of Protestants than they are of them. The negative images that they have of each other are centered on religious tolerance. However, White Catholics have more negative views about Jews than they do about Protestants, and this is associated with business practices. White Catholics were perceived by Black Protestants favorably but less so by Jews.

JEW: This group is the least critical of other groups.

> The Jews were somewhat less critical of the Protestants than were the Catholics, and they were also somewhat less critical of the Catholics than were the Protestants. This relatively favorable image was reciprocated by the White Protestants but not by the Catholics, who were much more critical of the Jews than of the Protestants.[8]

All other groups criticize this group.

> The Negro [sic] Protestants resembled the Catholics far more than the White Protestants so far as their image of the Jewish group was concerned. This image was a highly critical one: in the frequency with which criticism was expressed it was second only to the White Protestant image of the Catholic group.[9]

BLACK PROTESTANT: The focus is the images that Whites had of Black people. Three questions were put to Whites:

> Should White and Negro students attend the same or separate schools? Would they be "at all disturbed or unhappy" if a Negro with the same income and education moved into

---

7. Lenski, *Religious Factor*, 66.
8. Lenski, *Religious Factor*, 68.
9. Lenski, *Religious Factor*, 68.

their block? And if the answer was yes, "what would make them disturbed or unhappy?"[10]

Middle-class Whites in Detroit were concerned about integrated neighborhoods. Working-class Whites were unhappy about integrated schools.

> *Of the three White socio-religious groups, Catholics were the most likely to be disturbed by Negroes moving into their neighborhood, with 58 per cent expressing this view. White Protestants followed closely, with 53 per cent. Among the Jews, only 19 per cent said that they would be disturbed or unhappy.*[11]
>
> *. . . a third of the Catholics and Protestants expressed a preference for segregated schools, but only 8 per cent of the Jews.*[12]

Just to summarize, the research literature shows that there is a relationship between church membership and racial prejudice. Churchgoers who are less committed to the ideal of the Christian faith tend to be more racially prejudiced than those who attend out of conviction, or who do not attend at all. By far the majority of these studies relate specifically to the American situation. However, the Bagley study investigated this topic within the British context. A similar pattern emerged as to the nature of racial prejudice and church membership. Bagley identifies churchgoers who are members of the Church of England as among the most racially prejudiced in British society. So, a high level of religiosity meant a corresponding high level of racial prejudice.

There are other studies that differentiate church membership into types of engagement,[13] and there are studies relating measures of religious activity to measures of racial prejudice.[14] Researchers distinguish between sub communities and associational

---

10. Lenski, *Religious Factor*, 71.
11. Lenski, *Religious Factor*, 71.
12. Lenski, *Religious Factor*, 73.
13. Allport and Ross, "Personal Religious Orientation."
14. Gorsuch and Aleshire, "Christian Faith and Ethnic Prejudice."

aspects of religious groups, and the sub-community is not simply a by-product of the associational.[15] They come out of religious association, but they do not depend upon association for their existence. It is the sub-community group membership rather than the associational that is linked with racial prejudice. In other words, it is the sub-communities, not the churches, that can be described as intolerant and narrow-minded.

This research demonstrates that socio-religious subcultures are important because they represent the sum total of solutions to political and economic problems encountered by socio-religious groups in both their associational and subcultural form. Thus, subcultures reflect the experience of sub-communities. However, the social character of subcultures is influenced by a number of factors, including the theology and ideology of socio-religious groups, which go beyond the immediate social and economic need. The purpose of these studies was to find out what influence different types of religious commitment had had on secular institutions.

The American studies suggest a proportional correlation between the level of religiosity and racial prejudice, and that is supported by English surveys.[16] When highly committed church members were surveyed, they were found to be more tolerant, more able to stand in a critical stance toward the dominant culture of oppression. Thus, they were able to distance themselves from the dominant value system. What seems crucial in determining the different reactions and opinions of the two groups was the degree to which a Christian espoused the ideology of Christianity.

The research literature does seem to show that there is a correlation between church membership and racial prejudice. Churchgoers who have little intellectual or spiritual basis for any praxis are by far the most racially prejudiced. Committed enthusiasts and those who never attend church are more racially inclusive. This requires an analysis of religion and ethnic diversity to be carefully sensitive to the forms and modes of religious expression that may distinguish communal and associational religiosity and,

15. Lenski, *Religious Factor*.
16. Bagley, "Relation of Religion."

in the context of this book on the religious press of the Church of England, points to the inherent danger that may arise when Christianity is constructed as an element of English ethnicity.

Black Political Activism

The next section of this chapter is concerned with my understanding of the significance of Black theology as a critique of the way global majority people are framed in the religious press. Through an appreciation of the role of Black theology and its challenge to White majority churches, I hope to be able to offer a theological appreciation of the racialization process that marginalizes Black and Asian Christians. So where do we start with our discussion? The origins of Black theology in the British context can be found in Black political activism and in the politics of defensive confrontation starting in the 1960s and culminating in the popular uprisings of the 1980s and 1990s. We can trace these developments through an historical understanding of the sociological perspectives available at the time. The principal approach was that of political economy, which not so much replaced but overlapped the earlier models of ethnography and social reform. This will involve an analysis of formal and informal associations and an understanding of Black political leadership during that period.

A study of Sparkbrook, Birmingham, by Rex and Moore shifted the emphasis of research away from immigrant adjustments to the host society and toward a model of worker exploitation.[17] Using a Weberian model of market inequality, they placed the study of racial minorities within a class analysis rooted in the historical continuities of colonialism.[18] This involved an understanding of the role of conflict in competing for scarce resources such as housing. "Race" and ethnic relations researchers working within a class perspective had seen migrant workers as a sub-proletariat,[19] as

---

17. Rex and Moore, *Race, Community and Conflict*.
18. Rex and Tomlinson, *Colonial Immigrants in a British City*.
19. Gorz, "Immigrant Labour."

part of a fragmented but theoretically indivisible European working class,[20] as a segmented class faction,[21] and as a separate underclass.[22] Paul Gilroy tells us that the theoretical thinking behind the Marxist term *sub-proletariat* encouraged Black activists to open a dialogue with the White left, while directing their energies toward the development of relatively autonomous Black political activity.[23] This allowed Black socialists a means to retain a link with class theory as a positive change agent.

The Marxist approach can be contrasted with the Weberian model. The important difference between these two approaches lies in the way that Black people in Britain were seen as being subject to particularly intense forms of disadvantage and exploitation. For the Weberian, an underclass state results from the accumulated effect of losing struggles for market resources such as jobs, housing, and education. For the Marxists on the other hand, racial structurization is imposed by capital, and the emphasis is on the effect of production relations. State institutions further complicate it and seek to control labor power in the interest of capital. Castles and Kosack, who stressed that immigrants were part of the class structure of British capital, take this view. They conclude that the ruling classes in Europe actively manipulated the concept of "race" in order to divide the working class and thus rule.[24] It cannot be denied that capitalism benefits when workers are divided as they were in the 1974 Imperial Typewriters dispute in Leicester, where White dominated unions refused to intervene on behalf of Black workers. Capitalism requires racism not for racism's own sake but for the sake of capital.[25] Thus to attack racism is to attack capital. Any self-respecting and vocal Black theologian therefore is going to have to learn to argue, on several fronts at once. The whole business of using the gospel means undermining capital, means

20. Castles and Kosack, *Immigrant Workers and Class Structure*.
21. Miles and Phizacklea, "Class, Race Ethnicity," 491–507.
22. Rex, "Black Militancy and Class Conflict."
23. Gilroy, *There Ain't No Black*.
24. Castles and Kosack, *Immigrant Workers and Class Structure*.
25. Sivanandan, *Communities of Resistance*.

returning to the principals of jubilee and the communal aspirations of the early church. This takes us directly into the realm of social action, linking into the thoughts of liberation theologians like Gutiérrez.[26]

It is true that Marxism per se is fundamentally opposed to religious activity and proclivity of any kind. This can sit uneasily with Black thinkers as religion is so central to much of the Black experience. However, I cannot see why the analytical tools of one system cannot be applied to another context where they are helpful, which was the argument of many of the liberation theologians in their heated debate with the Vatican on this very issue. If we look at the intellectual debates of the time, and I did at the time take these on board, according to Rex there was no way into the British social system other than through membership of its class structure. Since newcomers usually had to start at the bottom, the exploitation of Asian and Black workers can be analyzed in terms of the extent to which racial and ethnic minorities gain acceptance in the working class and enjoy the same rights and privileges as White workers. Having examined the relationship of Black immigrants to the housing market, the labor market, and the education system, Rex concludes that what he was seeing was the formation of the immigrant underclass that was cut off from the main class structure of British society.[27] The term *underclass* was used by Myrdal to describe the unemployed at the bottom of a society. In Western industrial societies, immigrants and indigenous Black people fulfill a psychological function as a scapegoat group for those economically above them.[28] This stigmatization was an important element in the definition of the immigrant situation. However, the underclass is not an inherent mass characterized by a ghetto mentality or culture and unable to organize or act in its own class interest.[29]

---

26. See Gutiérrez, *Theology of Liberation* and *Power of the Poor in History*.
27. Rex, "Black Militancy and Class Conflict."
28. Baran and Sweezy, *Monopoly Capital*.
29. Rex and Tomlinson, *Colonial Immigrants in a British City*.

According to David Pearson most West Indians and Asian workers can be heuristically defined as an underclass so far as Black workers invariably have inferior life chances as compared to the native workers in a variety of market situations.[30] However, it is also the opinion of this researcher that such a view does not preclude the possibility of some degree of economic and social differentiation within ethnic and racial minorities. With respect to class, while Black workers may share a common social class background, we must also consider internal distinctions, such as the cultural and geographical divisions between various ethnic groups, for example, as well as other important regional, linguistic, and religious differences. Furthermore, a small but significant sector of Black workers have obtained equal or superior positions to some White workers.

There were three ways in which Black people could attempt to improve their disadvantaged position in British society. Firstly, they could organize themselves as members of an economic class and become incorporated into the traditional class structure of British politics. Secondly, Black people could set up ethnic organizations and engage in pressure group politics to obtain improved conditions. Thirdly, Black people could organize themselves as Black people irrespective of ethnic origin. Miles and Phizacklea referred to these three approaches as the class unity process, the ethnic organizations process, and the Black unity process.[31] According to Rex, formal associations such as trade unions, political parties, and immigrant associations represent groups of individuals who are bound together through sharing a common set of cultural meanings, norms, and beliefs which structure the social forms within which they interact.[32] These organizations are a pure form of association and can perform the functions of overcoming social isolation, affirming beliefs and values, and goal attainment. Rex draws distinction between these formal organizations and informal structures by demonstrating

30. Pearson, *Race, Class and Political Activism*.
31. Miles and Phizacklea, *Racism and Political Action*, 12.
32. Rex, "Black Militancy and Class Conflict."

that the latter involves a greater number of personalized and what he calls primary relationships.[33] Primary relationships are found in communities where people are bound together by intimate personal ties such as family kinship relationships or friendship networks. These groups are loosely structured and may meet in lodging houses, in pubs, or on street corners.

Rex believed that the Black political movements in Britain were moving toward a posture of defensive confrontation. Not having the protection of the trade union movement, and faced with high levels of youth unemployment, Black workers were organizing themselves communally in order to challenge the structures of White society. Rex told us that these groups often use violent rhetoric and talk of war with the system that oppresses them. He concludes that the politics of defensive confrontation in the long run may not prevent the entry of Black people into the working class, but rather it is an essential pre-condition for that entry.[34] The so-called riots in the summer of 1981 and the autumn of 1985 suggest that Rex had underestimated the strength of feeling with the Black community and the extent of which its anger would not be limited to the realms of rhetoric. From a Christian perspective there can be no advocacy or justification for violence on our streets. However, we have to try to understand the actions of desperate people who have also been the victims of violence.[35] Therefore, if there was little evidence of an autonomous Black theology emerging within the Black community, there is on the contrary ample evidence of the emergency of a secular politics of resistance.

Trevor Carter writing in the late 1980s argues that up until 1977 the Black community in Britain felt it was very much on its own against racist abuse and attack, without any appreciable support from the left and labour movement.[36] When support was forthcoming, it was in the form of the Anti-Nazi League. As a single-issue campaign centered on electoral politics, the anti-Nazi

33. Rex, "Black Militancy and Class Conflict," 83–86.
34. Rex, "Black Militancy and Class Conflict," 91.
35. Isiorho, "Faithful Cities and Their Theology," 101–5.
36. Carter, *Shattering Illusions*.

League modeled itself on the campaign for nuclear disarmament. The league was essentially anti-Nazi rather than anti-racist, although anti-racism was also part of its brief. The emphasis of the campaign was to protect White liberal democracy from organizations like the National Front, not Black people from racist attacks. This signaled to Black people that here again was another White organization, which in its attempt to be broad based had overlooked the needs and demands of Black people. Paul Gilroy believed that the Anti-Nazi League in the late 1970s used nationalism as part of its broad anti-fascist campaign by exposing the National Front as sham patriots who soiled the British flag.[37] It took Thatcher's defeat of Labour in 1979 to drive the left into its first serious examination of the identity and whereabouts of the working class and to accept that it was not all White and male.

Carter draws our attention to the importance of caucusing to ensure that White organizations to which Black people also belonged are more fully informed and answerable to their membership.[38] A Black caucus inside a White organization is not to be equated with separatism, since, by definition, it assumes a corporate membership of the wider body. However, the right of Black people to caucus has often been met by fierce resistance. The largely White leadership saw Black activists inside the Labour Party campaigning for Black sections as divisive and sectarian. However, there was no unanimity among Black people over the need for Black sections in the Labour Party, and for this reason the leadership was able to manipulate the differences in perspective.

Black Theologians

If the labour movement may be reasonably implicated in the reproduction of a xenophobic English ethnicity, then it is necessary to examine the significance of theological reactions to this phenomenon. One response crucial to a book on how Black and

---

37. Gilroy, *There Ain't No Black*, 131.
38. Carter, *Shattering Illusions*, 72.

Asian people are seen through the pages of *The Church Times* and *The Church of England Newspaper* is to give serious consideration to the emergence of a heterogeneous Black theology in the British context. Our starting point is the contribution of Robert Beckford, because he of all Black theologians is the most widely known on account of his engagement with popular media. However, I do not credit Beckford as the initiator or founder of Black theology in the UK. This role can be more appropriately assigned to Emmanuel Lartey as the first editor of *Black Theology* in Britain and convener of the Black Theology Forum in Birmingham.

Robert Beckford, if not the founder, can certainly be thought of as the herald of Black British theology in the UK. In looking at the White world with critical eyes, Beckford in *Dread and Pentecostal*[39] does not shrink from applying the same limpid gaze to the Black world. He openly acknowledges, with repentance, the oppressive structures, views, and practices within the Black churches. He addresses related issues of liberation such as sexism, classism, homophobia, and attitudes to people perceived as disabled. This makes for a coherent and holistic worldview that is wide-ranging and deeply refreshing.

One response critical to this study is the emergence of a heterogeneous Black theology. According to Hood, American Black people took the burden of their own liberation upon themselves.[40] They looked afresh at the doctrines of creation and then began a dialogue between their Christian and African inheritance. Their religious practices included adapting African culture, e.g., the ring shout. The potency of Christ the Liberator shone through the pernicious cloaking of White interest to give American Black people a sense of their own worth and validity. This negating of their own negation has had a profound effect, expressed in political and civic actions. They claimed their right to be children of God, a God who made them, loved them, redeemed them, suffered with them and had never forgotten them.

---

39. Beckford, *Dread and Pentecostal*.
40. Hood, *Begrimed and Black*.

According to James Cone, Black theology as a concept has its origin in the late 1960s when a group of radical Black clergy in the United States "began to reinterpret the meaning of the Christian faith from the standpoint of the black struggle for liberation." Their task was to theologize from within the Black experience, to interpret or make sense of "the meaning of God's liberating presence in a society where blacks were being economically marginalized."[41] This theology asks, "What does it mean to be black and Christian?" It also confronts White churches with their racism.

Cone identifies three major contexts of the origin of Black theology:[42]

The civil rights movement and Martin Luther King. A Black theology that rejected racism and affirmed the black struggle for liberation, this theology had its roots in the resistance to slavery. A theology that relates the Christian gospel to the struggle for racial justice was not well received by the White churches.

The publication of Joseph Washington's Black Religion *(1964).* Black theology was a rejection of this book and of the idea that the White churches had a monopoly on Christianity. If God is a God of justice and truth, then it is the Black church that is truly Christian, identifying the gospel with the struggle for justice.

The Black Power movement and Malcolm X. On July 31, 1966, the *New York Times* published a statement from the National Committee of Negro Churchmen (NCNC) which declared that "all people need power, whether black or white. We regard it sheer hypocrisy or as a blind and dangerous illusion the view that opposes love to power. Love must be the controlling element in power, not power itself. So long as white churchmen continue to moralize and misinterpret Christian love, so long will justice continue to be subverted in this land." According to Cone, this Black Power statement "initiated the development of a theological consciousness that separated radical black Christianity from the religion of white churches."[43]

41. Cone, *For My People*, 5.
42. Cone, *For My People*, 6–11.
43. Cone, *For My People*, 1.

Black theology has not confined itself to a critique of White churches. It has criticized the conservative posture of Black churches who refuse to do anything about racism and prefer to talk about heavenly freedom in the world to come. Some of these Black churches became indistinguishable from White churches as their clergy tried to copy the religion of Billy Graham and sometimes even that of the Moral Majority.

The church of the 1960s began to forget its mission of liberation. Cone comments thus:

> To preach the gospel without asking about its precise meaning for our time and situation is to distort the gospel.... A religion of liberation demands more than preaching, praying, and singing about the coming eschatological kingdom of God. It demands a critical theology based on the Bible and using the tools of the social sciences so that we can participate more effectively in establishing the kingdom in this world that we believe will be fully consummated in the next.[44]

Black theology emerged from the Black church and was a way of the Black church criticizing itself in order to be a more effective agent of liberation. It is a prophetic voice calling upon the Black church to reorder its priorities and to focus upon poor Black people in the inner cities rather than to follow the White churches into the suburbs.

Wilmore and Cone identified several immediate concerns.[45] They called for the Black church to make a commitment to establishing freedom schools that would offset the omissions and failings of the white-centered public school system. They wanted to see workshops set up to foster Black family solidarity. They pressed the urgency for training for lay leaders in community skills. They wanted great and serious efforts to support with concrete financial aid all those Black groups working for self-realization. And, most fundamentally, they insisted upon the removal of all images that suggest and reinforce the notion of God as White.

44. Cone, *For My People*, 120.
45. Wilmore and Cone, *Black Theology*.

Black theology had this task of calling the Black church back to its liberating heritage. By the 1970s, Black theology had also begun to lose its way. In some places it had become purely an academic discipline taught in universities and seminaries. By the end of the 1970s, there was a new interest in liberation theology, which was earthed in the struggle of the poor and had its focus in Latin America. Sadly, the Black church had got used to living without a Black theology and the self-examination that goes with it. Some Black churches became anti-intellectual and rejected theology while others used White seminaries to train their ministers.

Somehow Black theology and the Black church had to be reunited. Cone suggests a shared goal in the liberation of the Black poor. He comments thus:

> We must ask not what is best for the survival of black churches or black theology, but rather what is best for the liberation of the black poor in particular and the poor of the world in general. Unless we black preachers, theologians, and lay persons are prepared to measure our commitment to the gospel in terms of our participation in the liberation of the poor, then our gospel is not good news to the poor but instead an instrument of their oppression. . . . To think that we can do black theology apart from the black churches is sheer theological nonsense. And if we do not return to black churches with the intellectual humility and openness to be taught as well as to teach, then black churches should not listen to anything we say.[46]

So is Beckford doing the pioneering work of Black theology advocated by Cone? The church certainly needs to reclaim the true identity of the historical Jesus. It also needs to do its theology from starting with the context of people's lives, examining and changing the concrete daily realities. For God is not distant and Jesus has not gone away. Beckford sees Rasta thinking as a paradigm for Black rethinking of the Christian tradition, a way of receiving through Black experience, using all the powerful redemption evinced in

46. Cone, *For My People*, 116–17.

the liberating God who has inspired and rescued people out of unimaginable anguish. He believes that using popular culture is a valid way into doing theology. But can Beckford posit a genuine Christology and real theology in the heart of Bob Marley's songs? There is something about Marley's social and moral context that may give some of us pause for thought here.

Dread and Pentecostal will be read by some as a sequel to the earlier work *Jesus Is Dread*,[47] where Beckford writes from the perspective of a Black man, worshiping in the Black Pentecostal tradition, politically radical and liberal, while working in the heart of the White Church institution as a tutor in Black theology at the Queen's Foundation for Ecumenical Theological Education in Birmingham. The theological frame for this approach is the "not yet" eschatological approach rather than the "now" of kingdom theology. Beckford argues for a middle way between the two poles of combative struggle and submissive piety and citing the tough love of Martin Luther King in *Strength to Love*. He sees himself as working in "the master's house" in Queen's Theological College, teaching his students a balanced and tactical approach to resistance, while acknowledging the lure of the clear appeal of the combative perspective. For this combative paradigm drives the struggle and the struggler to the margin, which necessitates the constructive of a positive and powerful Black identity.

After an intelligent and informed discussion of the background and influences in Black Christianity, Beckford reviews the English response to the newcomers of the fifties and sixties. He notes that the Island Black Christians were very White minded:

> Hence, for a large number, warmth, welcome and acceptance would have been adequate compensation for the exclusive practices inherent in the White Church. In fact, where welcomes were warm and ministers sensitive, Black people generally stayed put.[48]

---

47. Beckford, *Jesus Is Dread*.
48. Beckford, *Jesus Is Dread*, 11.

A particular prophetic role for the Black church is glimpsed behind some of his statements. He writes about the internal and external dimensions of liberation. He refers to Christianity as a religion that is essentially a struggle against oppression.

> *Being committed to social justice is about asking questions and taking risks, so that we can alter the structures and systems that oppress us. This is the task of a Black Christian politics of liberation.*[49]

As Beckford identifies and defines Black cultural practices, he also deplores the appropriation of many aspects of Black culture into mainstream churches. Graham Kendricks, the hymn writer, is cited as someone who has stolen riches because he does not openly credit his sources and inspirations. This surreptitious use of blackness is profoundly alienating.

> *Because their Churches ignore Black liturgies, many Black Anglicans and Methodists are alienated in their worship setting. Some are simply patronized by the occasional rendition of a "spiritual" or a calypso-based church song from the Caribbean—usually sung in the wrong key and to the wrong beat. This form of cultural racism is usually justified in the name of tradition.*[50]

Beckford is a realist who focuses upon the future; no retrospective self-indulgence here.

> *Mobilizing our history is not therefore simply a return to all things African: it also involves taking seriously our intersection with European and North American cultures.*[51]

Beckford takes seriously the view of the church as the center and way of life for the Christian community. It has been said that the gospel makes anyone an alien in their own culture for it calls us to stand in prophetic opposition to the world, and he has clearly taken this on board.

---

49. Beckford, *Jesus Is Dread*, 13.
50. Beckford, *Jesus Is Dread*, 36.
51. Beckford, *Jesus Is Dread*, 37.

> *We must see the Church as a radical institution offering a countercultural and alternative existence. For Black Churches to become radical institution means finding new ways of enthusing them with the kind of independence of thought and radical praxis which are at the roots of their formation.*[52]

One of the things that makes the book so interesting to read is the way that Beckford draws upon his own experience. For example:

> *It's amazing when I think about it now! As a child, I never thought that White people were truly Christian. I was indoctrinated by the conversations of Black adult Christians to believe that our spirituality was better than the cold, staid and unwelcoming experience of White Christianity.*[53]

He goes on to add:

> *Because we were suspicious of White Christianity, we found it even more incredible that there were Black people in White Churches. . . . We also knew that many of them found it hard going. This was because many would worship with the White Church of Sunday morning and with the Black Church every Sunday evening.*[54]

Beckford then reviews Robinson Milwood's *Liberating Mission: A Black Experience*.[55] Milwood is a Black Methodist minister whose work exemplifies what Beckford calls the combative paradigm. This entails perceiving the church as a hostile place.

> *Its structures, practices and systems all reflect an ingrained commitment to White supremacy.*[56]

He develops this thus:

---

52. Beckford, *Jesus Is Dread*, 39.
53. Beckford, *Jesus Is Dread*, 42.
54. Beckford, *Jesus Is Dread*, 43.
55. Milwood, *Liberating Mission*.
56. Beckford, *Jesus Is Dread*, 47.

> Because the Church is a hostile place for Black people, the
> only legitimate response is protracted struggle—the second
> characteristic of the combative perspective.[57]

Being Black does not in itself mean that all Blacks are actively in the struggle. On the contrary, Beckford cites Milwood's suspicion of all other Black people:

> They are colonized until proven decolonized.[58]

Milwood thus argues that the combative perspective demands a prophetic spirituality. Beckford sees much to offer here but concludes:

> At its best, the combative approach is uncompromising in
> its critique of racism. It prioritizes an essentialist Blackness
> in the quest for racial justice. . . . At its worst, the combat-
> ive approach is victim to two failings: racial reasoning and
> the limitations of self-exile.[59]

Later he demonstrates how this approach works. He describes the covers of the Birmingham diocesan directory for two successive years in considerable detail.

> For some people, the cover of a diocesan directory is just
> a cover. For me the front cover of a diocesan directory is
> a bit like a record sleeve: it tells you something about the
> character of what you can expect inside.[60]

The 1996 cover had a photograph of the six-foot-tall bishop of Birmingham in purple looking down upon a very small Black girl of five or six years old against a background of a school building. It does not take a finely honed mind to detect the obvious resonances behind such an image.

> Such imagery has a history. The annals of colonial history
> are littered with images of White power and domination

---

57. Beckford, *Jesus Is Dread*, 48.
58. Beckford, *Jesus Is Dread*, 49.
59. Beckford, *Jesus Is Dread*, 49.
60. Beckford, *Jesus Is Dread*, 108.

over "native" peoples. Hence, this 1996 image harks back to an age of colonial domination and Black subjugation.[61]

He adds:

> *If size signifies power, then it is clear who is in control here. Symbolically, I would contend that the young girl signifies the Black Anglican presence within the diocese: small, curious and problematic to those in power.*[62]

The cover for the following year, 1997, depicts a blonde grandmother and child lighting a candle in a church. It has a Madonna-like appeal and communicates purity and piety. It is also powerfully White and completely unrelated both to the historical Jesus and to the diverse residents of the diocese. Beckford rightly asks, "Is this Christianity?"[63] As he decodes these images against a frame of the under-representation of Blacks within the diocesan structures and the lack of active promotion and nurture of Black vocations, both lay and ordained.

Beckford calls for change, roundly stating:

> *Liturgy and church life must identify and challenge the psychologically damaging effects of White supremacy, and must also engage in the Black community's struggle for political mobilization.*[64]

For our purposes here, we will treat *Jesus Is Dread* and *Dread and Pentecostal* as companion volumes which take as their implicit objective the need to demonstrate that Black Christians are diverse. Beckford never exactly says this, but it appears that he understands that the ad hoc treatment of persons as one group can simplify their oppression as a process. Beckford believes that Black Pentecostalism can provide a means to achieve emancipation-fulfillment. He looks at worship style and at culture, hence his theology is an attempt to reclaim for Britain the powerful force

---

61. Beckford, *Jesus Is Dread*, 108.
62. Beckford, *Jesus Is Dread*, 109.
63. Beckford, *Jesus Is Dread*, 110.
64. Beckford, *Jesus Is Dread*, 148.

for rebellion that was Christianity for the African slaves forcibly exported to the Americas. In *Jesus Is Dread* a particular prophetic role for the Black church is glimpsed behind some of his statements. He refers to Christianity as a religion that is essentially a struggle against oppression. In *Dread and Pentecostal* this becomes explicit in a discussion of a Dread Pentecostalism as a contextual and political theology able to articulate the life questions that pertain to Black experience, Black identity, and the Black church. All of which, we are told, relates to and is reflected in the reproduction of idea and the conventions of understanding which are located within the context of a faith community.

Black Pentecostalism is politicized and conscientized then by Dread which is the driving force of this theology. It relates ideas of "race" and gender to the context of where and how we live. Thus, there is a reading strategy and as such an interpretative process that betokens our encounter with the Bible and its implications for liberation. Not all reading strategies are radical, and it is the purpose of Dread Pentecostalism to challenge institutions to politicize reading agendas. There is also a need to form alliances and dialogue with other reading conventions. Dread itself occupies a place between Rastafarianism and Christianity.

We need now to ask some fundamental questions about Dread and Dread Pentecostalism in particular with regard to its standing as a viable theological construct for the Black church. Dread, on the one hand, and Pentecostalism, on the other, are separate systems of thought that are as diverse as each other. And to claaim a theological connection between them involves Beckford in a serious re-working of both. Dread Pentecostalism is put forward as a liberation theology whose origin is to be found in African Caribbean history. It is a political system that draws its strength from African Caribbean Christian experience. The focus, however, is Dread as a living existential reality of being Black and, as such, finding one's true identity in blackness as the concrete nature of that reality. This leads us to ask an important question: Does Dread Pentecostalism really represent an anti-essentialist, post-modern blackness? And if not, what type of theology is this? Clearly it can be described as a meta-narrative that demands equality without losing the politics of difference. However, it could be argued that Beckford does not so much sit on the fence that divides essentialist and non-essentialist understandings as negotiate the tightrope stretched between them. He talks here of a *strategic essentialism* which allows the Black church to experience Dread without losing its Christian focus and thereby turning Black Pentecostalism into a radical change agent. It is unclear whether this theology is descriptive of what is already happening in the Black church or whether this is a desired and future outcome. It is clear, however, that Beckford believes that the Black church needs this radical input from Dread while acknowledging its origins have more to do with Rastafarianism than with Christianity.

Dread stands for rebellion and resistance to oppressive structures. There is an inbuilt assumption that this makes it a prophetic theology. He vigorously both defends and explains the Black wisdom tradition, drawing on some of the hermeneutics of liberation theology to issue his call. My criticism here is that Beckford does not takes seriously enough his own argument that the church is the center and way of life for the Christian community. Beckford has not really taken on board how profound the dissonance ought to be between Christians and the world. We are left then with some practical questions about how Beckford will operationalize the concept of Dread within Pentecostalism. Prim and proper Black church members are unlikely to be enthused by funky Dread. White churches in suburbia are equally unlikely to adopt punk rock as their source of inspiration. Dread has been assigned a pivotal role within Pentecostalism. But what of its universality? Are there no ecumenical aspects to its functioning? I can but wonder, from an Anglican perspective, what effect Dread could have upon the Church of England where the convention is as much a signifier of Englishness as it is of theism. What are the implications here for emancipation fulfillment when the relationship between a church and its Black members is determined by a political agenda that has its origin in English ethnicity?

....

We now need to ask how the above relates to and is reflected in the British context through the lens of another Black theologian, namely Anthony Reddie, whose prolific and eclectic publications gave him accreditation as the principal sustainer and encourager of Black theology in the UK thirty years ago and at this present time. Reddie has great admiration for Beckford, who is to some extent a mentor for his early writing. However, in the process of locating Beckford, Reddie has raised two important questions that have implications for the very nature of Black theology itself. Firstly, Beckford's criticism of English liberalism is laudable, but he has also become dependent upon that constituent group more so than Pentecostalism as an arena for his work. It is this concern that leads Reddie to ask if Beckford has become perhaps by default the theologian for White people. Secondly, is Beckford doing Black theology or cultural studies, and how are they related? This question is not really answered, although Reddie does speculate as to what would have happened if James Cone had gone off to another discipline at a crucial time in the development of Black theology in the US.

So how do we locate the contribution of Anthony Reddie? I start then with where, I think, he is coming from. Reddie has argued that his story is not normative but that it does resonate with the second generation of Black Britons whose origins are Afro Caribbean and economically poor. He is a narrative theologian who uses the tools of archetypal story to highlight the underclass position of Black people at the hands of the failed promises of White churches and secular institutions. He is an active Methodist layperson who is critical of his church when he believes it to be in error and at the same time is able to celebrate its achievements in giving support to Black theology, which have included the funding of Black access courses at the Queens Foundation for Ecumenical Theological Education. The Methodist contribution to Black theology in Britain has also included the publication of Reddie's two-volume work *Growing into Hope: Christian*

Education in Multiethnic Churches[65] and the funding of a research fellowship at the Queen's Foundation.

Reddie warns against the popular idea that Black theology is any theology that is delivered by a Black person who happens to be a theologian. Black theology is always liberation theology because it is a discipline that attempts to make sense of Christianity as a process of liberation. Thus, it is also a theology for the Christian church in the sense that Black theology and the Black church should be engaged in the same liberation process, namely the conscientization of *ordinary Black people* and their empowerment to challenge oppression.[66] Reddie achieves this by working interactively with small groups in order to do his theology from the ground up. He is a participative centered Black theologian whose chosen method of working is clearly reflected in the presentation of accessible theology, which has been a strong theme throughout his published work. Reddie can also be described as a practical theologian whose form of Christian praxis gives focus to the social transformation of Black people and context that they inhabit. In this applied theology, he uses the tools of Christian education and social pedagogy. Black theology also draws upon the tools of Marxist analysis where appropriate but is never reducible to one particular socialist economic system. However, Reddie's theology can be located politically in a left-of-center position as a champion of the marginalized and oppressed and in complete opposition to patriarchy and racism.

For Reddie the starting point for Black theology is not necessarily the Bible or even the church but the experiences of Black people. However, the Bible and church are also important because they are part of that process that involves their re-imaging in the light of Black experience, which is the interpretive framework for this theology. Christology, the Bible, and the church remain core issues for Black theology because they are core issues for most Black Christians. Thus, doctrines and traditions have their place in the Reddie schema, but they are not written on tablets of stone

65. Reddie, *Growing into Hope*.
66. Reddie, *Working Against the Grain*.

nor are they a straitjacket to bind God's people. Black theologies are eclectic in nature, but they all have a clear focus in the centrality of Black experience and God's intervention and support of the down-trodden which goes beyond the historical text and further into an engagement with the Divine. It comes with no badge of acceptance from the White power structures whose system supports the structural poverty to found in capitalism.

According to Reddie, there has been a significant increase in support for Black churches in the UK and this has been largely unacknowledged by the White majority church. The Black church is not on the radar, and religious commentators talk about a UK Christianity that is exclusively White. Thus, the religious discourse in the UK is ethnocentric and the prevailing hegemony is not to ask questions about Black Christianity. So, what is going on? This rise in Black Christianity is happening at a time when the leaders of White majority churches are managing a decline in terms of both numbers of attending church services and in receiving crucial financial support to maintain the mission and ministry of their organizations. This crisis has also been seen in the production of literature that calls itself "mission shaped." However, where are the Black people in all of that?

. . . .

In seeking to understand this relationship between church and racial prejudice and its implications for Black theology in the contemporary British context, we turn now to *Rejection, Resistance and Resurrection* by Mukti Barton.[67] We have here a series of faithfully recorded stories that reflect the experience of racism for Black and Asian Christians in the Church of England. The origins of this work can be found in Black caucuses within the Diocese of Birmingham and beyond as those serious about the Christian faith speak out on racism in the Church. It is acknowledged by Black voices that racism with its long history of colonialism and slavery contradicts the Bible and the faith itself. The contributors,

67. Barton, *Rejection, Resistance and Resurrection*.

although rejected, have resisted racism and now tell their stories in the light of the resurrection hope of the gospel which has implications for the whole church of God. However, Barton makes the important point that this comes with a cost because speaking out on painful experience is to some extent to relive those experiences, but it is their wounds that speak also of resurrection.

For Barton it is Black theology that makes sense of these stories and is able to strengthen those engaged in struggle. The oppressed are not incapacitated by their oppression. Networking is crucial as a means of reinforcing the reality that all are made in the image of God and redeemed in the blood of Christ. Personal stories of rejection and of resistance become powerful narrative theology as the contextualized God talk of those who not only suffer but seek liberation from racial oppression. Concepts such as patriarchy, capitalism, militarism, sexism, racism, classism take on a new meaning, for those are empowered by a definite connection and consistency between their resistance to racism and the Christian gospel.

Barton concludes *Rejection, Resistance and Resurrection* with a discussion initiated by Malcolm X about the position of the house slaves being likely to acquiesce in their own oppression. Her starting point here is Robert Beckford's reflections on this subject, namely that these slaves can be likened to those who worship in their master's church, i.e., Black Anglicans. Barton understands Malcolm's position to contain a partial truth but believes the strategy of Black Anglicans who seek liberation has to be of a different kind from that of the field slaves, which is something Beckford also concedes. Black Anglicans will always challenge the master's church and make it their own because they articulate the struggle from the inside of that institution.

For Barton Black and Asian Christians are at the margins of a society that favors White people and disadvantages those who are considered outsiders. There is an internalization process going on which allows whiteness to understand itself as superior and having a legitimacy that allows it to dominate Black folk. The stories in *Rejection, Resistance and Resurrection* demonstrate clearly this internalized dominance on the part of White people in society at large and within historic White majority churches. This leads Barton to ask why they do this given the demands of the gospel to act so differently. She concludes that many White people are sleepwalking in a twilight zone between ignorance and knowledge and prefer at the end of the day to not rock the boat for fear of the consequences. An alternative way of looking at this at the institutional level is to say the Church of England is not asleep but rather pretending to be asleep. You wake up a sleeper, but someone who is pretending will just go on pretending.

Endnote

Our starting point was to evaluate the significance of organized religion and religious affiliations. The formation and expression of in-group and out-group sentiments clearly has an established presence in academic literature and can be seen in news items. US surveys suggest that churchgoers are likely to be more racially prejudiced than non-churchgoers. Thus, religiosity and racial prejudice were correlated. One of the jobs of Black theology is to clarify the pattern of attitudes that convey racism as seen in the relationship between racial prejudice and church membership, which is something we discussed earlier in this chapter. We need to reflect on this theologically as we consider the sociology of racial prejudice in our evaluation of racial bias to be found in the *Church Times* and the *Church of England Newspaper*.

A particular problem with the Church of England is that the conventional Christians who are actually hostile to the gospel are not necessarily on the margins as they may well be the people in charge. Churchgoers who have little intellectual or spiritual basis for any praxis are by far the most racially prejudiced. Committed enthusiasts and those who never attend church are more racially inclusive. *Faith in Church Newspapers* points to the inherent danger that may arise when Christianity is constructed as an element of English ethnicity and when the conventional Christians defend the institution from outsiders.

The Church report *From Lament to Action*,[68] considered only briefly in *Faith in Church Newspapers*, is about institutionalized racism. However, like previous reports it continues to see racism as a White sin which can be overcome with multiculturalism and racism awareness training. *From Lament to Action* struggles not to confuse personal relations with power relations, and the term *racism* seems to be used to cover all forms of racialized discrimination. In a review for *Black Theology* I describe this report as having a "slick and upbeat title," but with a style and language of a Church of England report.[69] From the start *From Lament to Action* anticipates its own failure—that it will be ignored by the institution of the Church of England just like previous reports. So where seriously is the challenge and the steer guiding the report? In short, what is the theology behind *From Lament to Action*? It has a view about theology as faith seeking understanding in the context of racialized exclusion, but this is something left to the Racial Justice Commission to take on board as a systemic and structural issue. So how can *From Lament to Action* identify or initiate *any urgency* in the need to effect change within the institution of the Church of England? Well, it wants the Church as an institution to create a standing committee of the Archbishops' Council which will oversee the work of the Racial Justice Directorate. *From Lament to Action* also advocates the introduction of new recruitment and appointments procedures.

To its credit, *From Lament to Action* does understand racial justice as the responsibility of the whole church and at the same time identify individual bodies within that institution with particular responsibility. These bodies need to be held to account for their inability to achieve the diversity required by the church. So, will *From Lament to Action* achieve anything? In my *Black Theology* review I speak as a parish priest with many years of experience and say that I for one will not be holding my breath.[70] At its strongest it seeks to shame the Church for not promoting

68. Archbishops' Anti-Racism Taskforce, *From Lament to Action*.
69. Isiorho, "From Lament to Action," 181–82.
70. Isiorho, "From Lament to Action," 181–82.

racial justice, but that presupposes the Church as an institution has some shame. I doubt that this will be an effective strategy for change. *From Lament to Action* recommends that the Church of England gives a higher profile to "race" and justice issues. The next chapter of this book will consider the ways in which *The Church Times* and *The Church of England Newspaper* may help or hinder the process of raising this profile.

Chapter Four

"Race," Ethnicity, and the Religious Press

Introduction

THERE WAS EVIDENCE TO support the idea that institutions tend to produce literature containing racialized frames of reference, even when those institutions are committed to racial equality. This is based upon a frame analysis that shows that only a minority of news items were concerned with "race" related issues or contained identifiable non-White actors. The lack of non-White actors as part of a framing process can be seen in the number of news items about non-White issues with no identifiable non-White people and the number of news items in which White actors discuss those issues (see appendix, table 1).

What I Found in the *Church Times* and the *Church of England Newspaper* during December 1990 and January/February 1991

In *The Church Times* we see that 3 percent of our sample contained news items with an explicit concern for "race" related issues and that 5.7 percent contained identifiable non-White actors. In *The Church of England Newspaper*, we see 3.4 percent of our sample contained news items with an explicit concern for "race" related issues and that 9.1 percent contained identifiable non-White actors. What the frame analysis shows is that, in both *The Church Times* and *The Church of England Newspaper*, only a minority of news items were concerned with "race" related issues or contained identifiable non-White actors. In this respect, both papers contained a frame of reference that tended to exclude non-White people or would only allow them to be visible or speak in the context of a non-White country.

No Identifiable Non-White Actors

In *The Church Times*, there were news items about non-White issues with no identifiable non-White actors, sometimes in the context of a predominantly non-White country, and less likely in the context of a predominantly White country. News items in the context of a predominantly non-White country, with no identifiable non-White actors, were news items about African countries. They usually contained information about what the West was going to do for them. For example:

> ST. AUSTELL TEAM[1]—This is a news item about how three parishioners from St. Austell, Cornwall, accompanied their vicar, Canon Andrew Matthew, to Uganda, where they conducted a mission in the Karamoja Diocese.

---

1. *Church of England Newspaper* 14.12.90, 5.

HUNGRY AFRICA[2]—This is a news item in which Peter Jennings surveys the crisis facing Africa and how aid is getting through to the famine-hit regions. A news item in the *Church Times*[3] was about how Christian Aid had made emergency grants totaling £621,000 to provide relief to millions of people facing starvation in Africa. We are told the grants will be used for food and transport in four countries whose names are not given.

In *The Church of England Newspaper* news items about non-White issues with no identifiable non-White actors in the context of a predominantly White country were about the Gulf War. They followed a "race" relations orientation. For example:

MUSLIMS REASSURED[4]—In this news item Church leaders reassured Muslims that the Gulf War need not harm Christian-Muslim relations in Britain.

In *The Church Times*, a news item in this category is as follows:

SPLIT OVER CONVENTION SITE[5]—It concerns the location of the 1991 General Convention of the Episcopal Church.

> *Affronted by the state of Arizona's rejection of a holiday honoring Martin Luther King Jr, Civil rights activists in the Episcopal Church are urging relocation of the church's 1991 general convention. It is at present scheduled to be held in July in Phoenix, the state capital.*[6]

The issue here is this: How can the Episcopal Church witness racial equality? The news item does quote the Church's Commission for Black Ministries, but there are no identifiable non-White actors.

2. *Church of England Newspaper* 18.1.91, 1.
3. *Church Times* 1.2.91, 3.
4. *Church of England Newspaper* 1.2.91, 3.
5. *Church Times* 14.12.90, 2.
6. *Church Times* 14.12.90, 2.

The majority of news items about non-White issues which contained no identifiable non-White actors were also news items in which White actors discuss those issues. In *The Church Times* there were seven news items in which White actors discussed non-White issues: two of these were in the context of a predominantly non-White country, while five were in the context of a predominantly White country. In the *Church of England Newspaper* there were fourteen news items in which White actors discussed non-White issues: nine in the context of a predominantly non-White country; and five in a predominantly White country.

News items which quoted White actors discussing non-White issues in a context of a predominantly non-White country were news items which rarely contained non-White actors. The exceptions of this were the following two news items, which featured both non-White and White actors.

GULF WAR HOPE FOR HOSTAGES[7]—This news item is about the Gulf War and the effects this might have upon the situation regarding the Western hostages. A pessimistic view is taken by Walid Jumblatt, the Lebanese Druze leader, and this is counteracted by a spokesperson at Lambeth Palace.

PATRIARCH CRITICISES OUTBREAK OF WAR[8]—A news item in which the Gulf War is discussed by Patriarch Rafael Ier Bidawid, of the Chaldean Church of Babylon and the secretary of the World Council of Churches.

News items which quoted White actors discussing non-White issues in a context of a predominantly non-White country included this news item:

AMERICAN CHURCH LEADERS TAKE A HARD "NO" WAR LINE[9]—This is a news item about the Gulf War in which Church leaders call for a United Nations–sponsored Middle East peace conference. Their concern is not

---

7. *Church of England Newspaper* 25.1.91, 1.
8. *Church of England Newspaper* 15.2.91, 5.
9. *Church Times* 28.12.90, 1.

exclusively the Gulf War. The conference would also deal with the occupation of the West Bank and Gaza Strip, Lebanon, and Cyprus. With the notable exception of Bishop Winton Anderson, moderator of the Black Church Liaison Committee of the World Council of Churches, the news item quotes White actors discussing the internal politics of the Middle East, which is essentially a non-White issue. The news item quotes, among others, Edmond Browning, the presiding bishop of the Episcopal Church of America, and Jim Wallace, the editor of *Sojourners* magazine in Washington, DC.

More typical of news items which quoted White actors discussing non-White issues in a context of a predominantly non-White country was

ERITREANS "THIRSTING TO DEATH"[10]—This was a news item in which a Christian aid worker returns to Britain after a month-long visit to Eritrea, monitoring emergency food distribution. Her conclusion is that the death of livestock will result in famine. How insightful can you get.

In *The Church Times*, news items which quoted White actors discussing non-White issues in a context of a predominantly White country, although not exclusively concerned with internal decision-making processes, were Church centered. Often these news items would start with a conversation or set of meetings but then broaden out into discussions which had implications for social policies beyond the confines of Church institutions. Typical of this group are these news items:

SPLIT OVER CONVENTION SITE[11]

US CHURCH WILL CARRY WITNESS INTO ARIZONA[12]

In *The Church of England Newspaper* news items in which White actors discussed non-White issues in a context of a

10. *Church of England Newspaper* 18.1.91, 16.
11. *Church Times* 14.12.90, 2.
12. *Church Times* 11.1.91, 2.

predominantly White country were news items dominated by the Gulf War and the implications that this would have for "race" relations at home. Typical of this group was this news item:

> CHRISTIAN DUTY TO FOSTER MUSLIM RELATIONS[13]— This was about the Reverend Janet Sowerbutts, moderator of the Thames North Province of the United Reformed Church, who urged Christians to be particularly concerned with maintaining contacts with Muslims and Jews during the Gulf War to help overcome misunderstandings.

Identifiable Non-White Actors Discussing Non-White Issues

Finally, we get to non-White actors allowed to discuss non-White issues. Here we have further support for the idea that institutions produce literature containing racialized frames of reference even when those institutions claim to be committed to racial equality. This is based on the data that shows only a minority of news items made it possible for those actors to discuss issues pertaining to their interests. In *The Church Times* and *The Church of England Newspaper* there were news items in which non-White actors discussed non-White issues usually in the context of a predominantly non-White country, and only occasionally in the context of a predominantly White country. The predominantly non-White countries in which non-White actors discuss non-White issues were those of the African continent and included South Africa, Sudan, Uganda, and Zambia. A news item called **WORLDWIDE LAUNCH FOR EVANGELISM**[14] continues this theme with the opinions of bishops of African countries who discuss the Decade of Evangelism as it pertains to their situation. The news items quote the Rt. Rev. Alpha Mohammed, bishop of Mount Kilimanjaro; Yona Okoth, the Ugandan archbishop; and

---

13. *Church of England Newspaper* 8.2.91, 3.
14. *Church of England Newspaper* 4.1.91, 16.

Bishop David Gitari from Kenya. In both papers, Black people were almost allowed to speak for themselves when the context was one of a predominantly Black country.

There was only one news item in which non-White actors discussed non-White issues in the context of a predominantly White country, entitled:

> ABORIGINAL REMINDER FOR WORLD COUNCIL[15]— This news item quotes Anne Pattel-Grey, the head of the Australian Council of Churches Aboriginal and Icelander Commission. She comments on the arrangements being made to draw attention to the Aboriginal origins of Australia at the Seventeenth Assembly of the World Council of Churches.

Clearly, there is a reluctance to allow non-White actors to speak in a context of a predominantly White country, and this is seen in the avoidance of political issues involving non-White people in Britain. A good example of this is the following news item:

> PLEA FROM WORLD'S MOST INDEBTED ISLE[16]—The news item focuses upon Rt. Rev. Neville de Soza's recent visit to England. We are told that the bishop has spent a fortnight campaigning on two issues close to his heart. The first of these is third-world debt. We learn that Jamaica has the highest per capita debt in the world and that the International Monetary Fund (IMF) places such conditions on the payment of loans that poverty and malnutrition are the result. The bishop says:
>
>> It's the IMF structural adjustment program that gives priority to paper concepts like *balance of payments* and *no trade barriers.*[17]

---

15. *Church Times* 7.12.90, 2.
16. *Church Times* 14.12.90, 2.
17. *Church Times* 14.12.90, 2.

Their effects on actual people, such as malnutrition, poverty, and crime, are ignored. We are also told that the bishop's campaign has been to arouse public awareness and to encourage protest. However, we are given no information as to how this campaign applies to the bishop's second concern, namely the alleged discrimination against people from the Caribbean by British immigration officials. This issue, close as it is to the bishop's heart, is not mentioned again.

In *The Church of England Newspaper*, this same story is still located in the context of a predominantly non-White country, but the bishop is allowed to say something about the British situation.

YOU HEAR FROM WHERE YOU STAND[18]—Here the Rt. Rev. Neville de Soza, bishop of Jamaica, discusses immigration controls and the position of Black people in the Church of England. The bishop says:

> *It is disappointing to people from the Caribbean who are brought up in the English Church (which was until recently the Church of England in Jamaica) and have participated with a sense of belonging and inclusion. Then we come to the Mother Church, and nobody seems to welcome you— you feel rejected.*[19]

The Framing of Non-White Actors

The frame analysis depicts how non-White actors are portrayed according to four contextual dimensions. These included a focus mainly on "race" relations; a focus mainly not on "race" relations; a focus on a predominantly non-White country or a predominantly White country (see table 1 in appendix). Typical of news items in the category of **"race" relations focus—non-White country** were

---

18. *Church of England Newspaper* 14.12.90, 6.
19. *Church of England Newspaper* 14.12.90, 6.

TUTU: KEEP SANCTIONS[20] in which Archbishop Tutu called for sanctions to continue against the South African regime.

SHARIA IN SUDAN[21]—This was a news item about the imposition of Sharia (Islamic) law in northern Sudan and how this might affect the mainly Christian south. The identifiable non-White actor is the Sudanese military leader, General Omar el-Bashire, who is reported to have said that the Christians would be allowed to choose their own legal system.

APARTHEID: "NO REWARD"[22]—This news item names Lula Xingwane as the director of women's ministries for the South African Council of Churches and coordinator for the Ecumenical Decade of Women in South Africa. The news item concerns the continuation of sanctions against the South African government.

The majority of news items that had identifiable non-White actors that were not about "race" relations in Britain were found to be within the developing world and the rest of the world. Typical news items in the category of **non "race" relations focus—non-White country** were focused on African countries, where Black actors were framed as problems and as passive recipients of Western help. Some of these news items focused on the mission activities of the West, while others were concerned with the Church and political issues of those countries. For example:

CMS COMMISSIONING[23]—A news item about the commissioning of mission partners to be "sent out" by the Church Missionary Society. The service was led by Bishop Michael Nazir Ali.

ANGOLANS WHO WOULD BE ANGLICANS "PUT OUT FEELERS" VIA MOZAMBIQUE[24]—In this news item,

20. *Church of England Newspaper* 15.2.91, 16.
21. *Church of England Newspaper* 1.2.91, 7.
22. *Church Times* 22.2.91, 2.
23. *Church of England Newspaper* 21/28.12.90, 3.
24. *Church Times* 18.1.91, 2.

the United Evangelical Church of Angola wants to join the Anglican Communion and has sought the help of the Rt. Rev. Dennis Sengulane, a bishop in Mozambique. However, the United Society for the Propagation of the Gospel (USPG), which, we are told, covers Mozambique, were puzzled to hear of these developments. The news item takes it for granted that missionary societies have a role to play in the initiatives taken by Black churches. It would seem that the Angolan Church has no intention of asking USPG for permission to join the Anglican Communion. It is interesting to note that in their duplicated sheet announcing their desire to join the Anglican Communion, the United Church of Angola makes it clear that their founder was an Anglican priest who had not been sent by a missionary society.

NEW AFRICAN HYMNS[25]—This news item was about the use of traditional African music in church worship. It quotes Andrew Muwowo, director of youth work in the United Church of Zambia, who wants to adapt traditional songs and use them in church.

SUDAN BISHOP'S FAMILY SURVIVES REBEL LOOTING[26]—This news item names the Rt. Rev. Joseph Morona, the bishop of Maridi, and the Rt. Rev. Daniel Zindo, bishop of Yambio, who, following political unrest, are unable to return home after they attend a bishops' meeting in Khartoum. The item also tells us that the Rev. Jonathan Manza and the Rev. John Abraham and their families had been taken away by rebel forces.

News items about the rest of the world were dominated by the Gulf War and the release of Western hostages. Typical of news items in this category were those where support was given for British bishops to use force against Saddam Hussein and what effect this might have upon the release of a small number of Western hostages. For example:

25. *Church of England Newspaper* 8.2.91, 7.
26. *Church of England Newspaper* 18.1.91, 2.

BISHOPS COUNTENANCE MILITARY ACTION BUT STRESS THE COST IN HUMAN SUFFERING[27]—In this news item bishops justify the use of force, albeit with a heavy heart, in order to oust Saddam Hussein from Kuwait.

INSTABILITY NOT HELPFUL TO HOSTAGES[28]—This news item is about Terry Waite and the other Western hostages. The big question is this: Will a Gulf War affect their release? The news item names Druze leader Walid Jumblatt and Hezbollah leader Hussein Mussawi, whose opinions are sought on this all-important question.

Not all of these news items were anti–Saddam Hussein, although he is usually the identifiable non-White actor. It is interesting to note that where Saddam Hussein is not the only identifiable non-White actor, he is less likely to be cast in the role of villain.

SPLIT OVER "JUST WAR" QUESTION WORLDWIDE[29]—This is a news item about divided opinions within the Anglican Communion as to whether the use of force against Saddam Hussein is just. This news item quotes the Rt. Rev. Samir Kafity, who says that it is not justified.

PATRIARCH CRITICISES OUTBREAK OF WAR[30]—In this news item Patriarch Raphael Ier Bidawid, of the Chaldean Church of Babylon, says that the war should never have been allowed to happen and that the Western media have presented a one-sided view of the conflict.

Typical of news items in the category of **non "race" relations focus—White country** was a news item entitled **APPOINTMENTS**.[31] It included the appointment of the Rev. David Shrisunder, from Kolahphur, North India, as priest-in-charge of Sinfin Moore Local Ecumenical Project, Derby.

27. *Church Times* 18.1.91, 1.
28. *Church Times* 25.1.91, 1.
29. *Church of England Newspaper* 25.1.91, 3.
30. *Church of England Newspaper* 15.2.91, 5.
31. *Church of England Newspaper* 21/28.12.90, 3.

ULVERSTON EMPHASIS[32]—This news item is about how the churches of Ulverston have launched the Decade of Evangelism in Cumbria. At their celebration event, the speaker was John Magumba, from Jinja, Uganda.

Also in this category was a news item without a headline and accompanying the photograph of the four presidents of the Church Together organization.[33] This included a Black Church leader, the Reverend Desmond Pemberton, the national superintendent of the Wesleyan Holiness Church.

Typical of news items in the category of **"race" relations focus—White country** were those in which non-White actors share the stage with White actors. Those news items were those concerning the Gulf War and Christian-Muslim relations.

UK RELIGIOUS LEADERS URGE INTERFAITH HARMONY AT HOME[34]—This was an item about the importance of good "race" relations in the light of the Gulf War in which five religious leaders in Liverpool issued a statement that encouraged interfaith harmony. The statement is signed by Akbar Ali, senior trustee, Liverpool Muslim Society; John New, Merseyside Free Church moderator; S. Safiruddin, president, Pakistani Association Liverpool; David Shepherd, bishop of Liverpool; and Derrick Warlock, (RC) archbishop of Liverpool.

BAND OF FRIENDSHIP[35]—In this news item the Rt. Rev. Michael Adie, the bishop of Guildford, assures Iman Ali Madani of the Woking Mosque of his concerns for good relations between Christians and Muslims during the Gulf War.

LEADERS MEET[36]—The Rt. Rev. Stanley Booth Clibborn, bishop of Manchester, meets Dr. Ahmed of the Manchester

---

32. *Church of England Newspaper* 4.1.91, 4.
33. *Church Times* 18.1.91, 3.
34. *Church Times* 1.2.91, 1.
35. *Church of England Newspaper* 22.2.92, 7.
36. *Church of England Newspaper* 1.2.91, 3.

Council of Mosques, at the central mosque in Manchester, to discuss the tensions created by the Gulf War.

Sometimes non-White actors challenge the system that oppresses them with the help of White actors. An example of this is a news item which contained no headline but a photograph of Nelson Mandela with Bishop Huddleston as an anti-apartheid veteran. In other items not only do White actors help Black actors to achieve their objectives, but they also take over completely and change those objectives. This is the case of news coverage of Britain where the focus of attention is no longer on challenging the system which oppresses. For example:

BISHOP: AFFIRM BLACKS[37]—This headline falls into the category of White actor positive predicate. The White actor, in this case a bishop, the Rt. Rev. Keith Sutton, bishop of Litchfield, affirms Black people who are the positive agents. This news item names two identifiable Black actors, President Jawara of Gambia in West Africa, and Mr. Taylor, a Black prospective MP, but it is the White actor who is dominant. It is he who has been to see another White actor, the prime minister, John Major. And he does this at a lunch held in honor of one of the Black actors, President Jawara. The subject of the discussion seems to be not only "race" relations in general but Black leadership, which the bishop believes to be important, but the news item goes on to discuss a Black actor, Mr. Taylor, who has experienced racist abuse at the hands of the Cheltenham Conservative Party. The bishop links the two issues together thus:

> *The good atmosphere of this lunch had earlier been strengthened by the new Prime Minister's outright rejection of the racist remarks from Cheltenham Spa, criticizing the selection of Mr Taylor, a black prospective MP (as a conservative candidate there).*[38]

37. *Church Times* 14.12.90, 4.
38. *Church Times* 14.12.90, 4.

News items in which non-White actors were in the background were also dominated by the Gulf War, but here the identifiable non-White actor is Saddam Hussein.

- ARCHDEACON OFFERS TO VISIT SCHOOL[39]—This was a news item in which the archdeacon of Stoke on Trent offers to visit schools in an initiative aimed at stamping out anti-Muslim feelings among young people. Christians are asked to befriend their Muslim neighbors as the war in the Gulf intensifies.

- BISHOP CRITICISES MP[40]—The Rt. Rev. John Davis, the bishop of Shrewsbury, criticizes Mr. Derek Conway, MP, for his view on the Gulf War. Mr. Conway has said in a local newspaper that the city of Baghdad should be razed to the ground by Allied forces.

- HAWKE COMPLIMENTS W.C.C.'S WORLD WORK[41]—Bob Hawke compliments the World Council of Churches, seeks to justify his government's position on Aboriginal rights, and defends the Allied policy in the war with Saddam Hussein.

Endnote

Only a minority of news items were ostensibly concerned with "race" related issues or contained identifiable non-White actors. Thus, institutions produce literature containing racialized frames of reference which have the effect of excluding people of global majority heritage. My second big idea was to suggest that the more evangelical the ecclesiology of an Anglican newspaper, the more racialized is its frame of reference likely to be. Thus, *The Church of England Newspaper*, being a more evangelical publication than *The Church Times*, would contain a more racialized frame of reference. We would expect the racialization process to

39. *Church of England Newspaper* 8.2.92, 3.
40. *Church of England Newspaper* 8.2.92, 3.
41. *Church of England Newspaper* 15.2.91, 5.

be reflected in items about significantly fewer non-White actors and for those actors to be framed in a context that was considerably more racialized than that of *The Church Times*.

The percentage of news items containing identifiable non-White actors was greater in *The Church of England Newspaper* than it was in *The Church Times*, as was the percentage of these news items occurring in a context outside that of "race" relations. Thus, in *The Church of England Newspaper* not only were there more non-White actors than in *The Church Times*, but they were also more likely to appear in a context independent of White people. Thus, the evangelical publication, which was expected to contain a more racialized frame of reference than *The Church Times*, actually contained a frame of reference that was less racialized. So, in this respect, the idea that the more evangelical the ecclesiology of an Anglican newspaper, the more racialized its frame of reference is likely to be, did not hold up. *The Church of England Newspaper*, although a more evangelical publication than *The Church Times*, did not contain a more racialized frame of reference. News items in *The Church of England Newspaper* were not racially framed in a way that was significantly different from that of *The Church Times*. There was a commonality of racialized framing in *The Church Times* and *The Church of England Newspaper*, which was greater than any difference between the two papers.

The lack of non-White actors in *The Church of England Newspaper* discussing non-White issues can be explained by the greater percentage of space in square centimeters given over to developing world news. Thus, in *The Church of England Newspaper*, there are more news items about non-White issues with no identifiable non-White actors, but there are also more news items set in the context of predominantly non-White countries. This also helps to explain why it is that in *The Church Times*, White people discussed non-White issues in the context of a predominately White country whereas in *The Church of England Newspaper* they did this in the context of a predominantly non-White country.

The findings in both newspapers show that news items about "race" related issues, and identifiable non-White actors, in the religious press of the Church of England have been racialized by a process of exclusion. This framing of exclusion also involves news items about non-White issues. More White actors were discussing non-White issues than non-White actors were discussing those issues. There was a neglect of political issues involving non-White people in British society. When non-White actors did appear, they were allowed to speak for themselves when the context was one of a predominantly non-White country.

What I Found in the *Church Times* and the *Church of England Newspaper* during December 2023 and January/February 2024

I looked at 166 news items in *The Church Times* and 146 in *The Church of England Newspaper*. This is more or less half the number of news items analyzed in the first part of this chapter for these papers. The reason for this is because the *Church of England Newspaper* is now a fortnightly publication, and I chose a sample from both papers that would reflect this change. This sample includes two papers for December 2023 and January and February 2024 for both *The Church Times* and *The Church of England Newspaper*.[42] Readers need to note that *The Church Times* has as many as 39 to 47 pages and that the Christmas edition in 2023 ran to 56 pages because it was a double edition including both 22 and 29 December. *The Church of England Newspaper* is usually 16 pages. Table 2 does not provide data on news items in which White actors discuss non-White issues or non-White actors discussing those issues as a separate category. This information can be found elsewhere in the table. Questions about whether a news item was an example of identifiable non-White actors discussing non-White issues or just a news item that happened to quote some non-White actors is something that needs further discussion and qualitative analyses. As in the first part of this chapter only a minority of news items

---

42. *Church Times* and *Church of England Newspaper*, 8 and 22 December 2023, 5 and 19 January 2024, 2 and 16 February 2024.

were ostensibly concerned with "race" related issues or contained identifiable non-White actors. *The Church Times* and *The Church of England Newspaper* continue to produce literature having racialized frames of reference which have the effect of excluding people of global majority heritage.

In *The Church Times* we see that 4.2 percent of our sample had news items with an explicit concern for "race" related issues and that 10.2 percent had identifiable non-White actors. In *The Church of England Newspaper*, we see 5.4 percent of our sample had news items with an explicit concern for "race" related issues and that 9.5 percent had identifiable non-White actors. What the frame analysis shows is that in both *The Church Times* and *The Church of England Newspaper*, only a minority of news items were concerned with "race" related issues (see table 2). There was a percentage increase in the number of news items with identifiable non-White actors for both papers.

More News Items about Non-White People without Them

Following the findings from the 1990–91 sample I now want to look at those news items in the contemporary period for *The Church Times* and *The Church of England Newspaper* concerning non-White issues with no identifiable non-White actors. Eight of these news items were in the context of a predominantly non-White country and three in the context of a predominantly White country. *The Church Times* had a greater number of these items (see table 2). Typical of these news items were as follows.

CCLA: FIRMS TALK MORE THAN ACT ON SLAVERY[43]—
This is a news item that gives focus to benchmarking from the sustainable investment company CCLA, who say that the top one hundred firms are all talk and little action when it comes to challenging modern slavery. Fifty million

43. *Church Times* 8.12.23, 7; note that this is not a categorically Black or non-White issue.

people are enslaved through the global operations and supply chains of modern capitalism and the human-rights abuses that this involves. Marks & Spencer and Tesco are singled out as consumer-facing business in the fight against modern slavery. This is a very informative news item in which benchmarking is based upon disclosures from these companies but lacks any comment from the recipients of these improved businesses practices.

WELBY: CLEAN ISLAMOPHBIA AND ANTI-SEMITISM OFF UK'S DOORSTEPS[44]—This is a news item in which the archbishop of Canterbury has free range to set out his views on the subjects of Islamophobia and anti-Semitism, which presupposes he has some special knowledge and expertise on both subjects. Islamophobia and anti-Semitism come across as interchangeable subjects in Welby's commentary. We are left with the idea that we really must wipe these sins off the Christian doorsteps of this nation, as if these issues had never had anything to do with the good folk of the UK. The news item tries to present some kind of balance to the disproportionate situation of the Middle East, a difficult thing to do with so many innocent people under fire in Gaza. The Palestinian peace activist Hamze Awawde does get a small say, but this news item is about important White people and their priorities.

BISHOP QUESTIONS RWANDA SCHEME IN LORDS' DEBATE ON HUMAN RIGHTS[45]—A news item in which the bishop of Durham, the Rt. Rev. Paul Butler, challenged the government's policy of sending asylum-seekers to Rwanda. As laudable as this protest is, there is nothing in the news item about how asylum-seekers feel about the abuse of their human rights. The news item does not have a response from asylum-seekers on the bishop's speech.

---

44. *Church Times* 8.12.23, 10.
45. *Church Times* 12/29.12.23, 6.

GAZA MOURNS AFTER AIR STRIKE HITS REFUGEES[46]—A news item about Gaza with no voices from Gaza.

CHRISTIANS ENCOURAGED TO JOIN IN WEEKLY MARCHES AGAINST GAZA WAR[47]—Another news item with no identifiable world majority voices.

CONGRESS CONDEMNS ANTI-ZIONISM[48]—A news item in which anti-Zionism is seen as synonymous with anti-Semitism. This news item has no challenge to this extreme position and makes it impossible for people to criticize, including world majority voices, the foreign policy of the modern state of Israel without being accused of racism. This is very poor journalism.

GAZA CONFLICT AND ANTI-SEMITISM BRINGS "WORLD TO BRINK" SAYS POPE[49]—A short news item in which Pope Francis backed the two-state solution of the Oslo process. Christian leaders express concern about the humanitarian catastrophe in Gaza but there is no voice from Palestinian leaders allowing them to speak for themselves in this news item.

MODERN SLAVERY TO BE ADDRESSED IN NEXT YEAR'S LENT RESOURCES[50]—This news item is about resources for a Lent course. There is a recognition that there are twelve million children trapped in modern slavery and that climate issues have a part in doing something to change this. There is a focus on the causes of injustice that leads to slavery but there are no voices from the vulnerable in this news item. Another news item with no identifiable non-White actor voices.

---

46. *Church Times* 05.1.24, 9.
47. *Church Times* 19.1.24, 10.
48. *Church of England Newspaper* 8/12.23, 5.
49. *Church of England Newspaper* 2.2.24, 5.
50. *Church of England Newspaper* 8/12.23, 4.

Identifiable Non-White Actors

My frame analysis depicts how non-White actors are portrayed according to contextual dimensions with or without a focus on "race" relations. Secondly, I wanted to know if this context was in a predominantly non-White or White country. As with our 1990–91 sample this interaction of dimensions gave a total of four different contexts in which non-White actors are framed: "race" relations focus in a non-White country; non "race" relations focus in a non-White country; non "race" relations focus in a White country; "race" relations focus in a White country. Typical news items in the category of a **"race" relations focus in a non-White country** were as follows.

VATICAN HELPS TO FREE NICARAGUAN CLERICS[51]—
This news item is about how the Vatican was able to negotiate with the Nicaraguan government the release of two bishops and seventeen priests. The clergy have been accused of supporting the people of Nicaragua in their campaign calling for the resignation of the government.

CHRISTMAS APPEAL FOR PEACE FROM HOLY LAND[52]—
This is a news item in which the patriarchs and heads of the churches in Jerusalem, including the archbishop of Jerusalem, call for peace in the Middle East. They talk about the horrors, misery, and sorrow to countless families caught in the present crisis.

> *Yet it was into such a world that our Lord himself was born in order to give us hope. Here, we must remember that during the first Christmas, the situation was not far removed from that of today. Thus The Blessed Virgin Mary and St Joseph had difficulty finding a place for their son's birth. There was the killing of children. There was military occupation. And there was the Holy Family becoming*

---

51. *Church Times* 19.1.24, 13.
52. *Church of England Newspaper* 5.1.24, 3.

displaced as refugees. Outwardly, there was no reason for celebration other than the birth of the Lord Jesus.[53]

200 CHRISTIAN VILLAGERS KILLED IN NIGERIA CHRISTMAS MASSACRES[54]—This news item is about a series of Christian massacres in Nigeria. It is about religious persecution leaving two hundred people dead and twenty thousand displaced in more than eighty communities. According to Timothy Nuwan, vice president of Church of Christ in Nations, to Agence France Presse, "many people were killed, slaughtered like animals in cold blood."[55]

BISHOPS CONDEMN GAZA KILLINGS[56]—This news item is concerned with the condemnation from European bishops of the killing of two nuns, Nahida Anton and Samar Antoun. This was an Israeli sniper attack on two Christian women in the compound of the Holy Family Church, Gaza. "The desecration of this compound and the destruction of the Sisters' Convent, signaled as a place of worship since before the beginning of the war, is profoundly disturbing."[57]

STEP FORWARD FOR PAKISTAN'S MINORITIES[58]—A news item in which Pakistani students will no longer have to do Islamic studies. According to Nasir Saeed this is a significant achievement and shift in Pakistan's education policy "in the struggle for equal rights and opportunities in the education sector."[59]

Typical news items in the category of a **non "race" relations focus in a non-White country** were as follows:

53. *Church of England Newspaper* 5.1.24, 3.
54. *Church of England Newspaper* 5.1.24, 4.
55. *Church of England Newspaper* 5.1.24, 4.
56. *Church of England Newspaper* 5.1.24, 4.
57. *Church of England Newspaper* 5.1.24, 4.
58. *Church of England Newspaper* 2.2.24, 5.
59. *Church of England Newspaper* 2.2.24, 5.

ETHIOPIAN CHURCHES AGREE TO FORM COUNCIL[60]—This news item reports on the formation of an ecumenical council of churches to include the Ethiopian Orthodox Tewahedo Church, the Ethiopian Evangelical Church Mekane Yesus, and the Ethiopian Catholic Church.

CHURCH LEADERS CONDEMN ISRAEL IN FURTHER CEASEFIRE CALL[61]—Faith leaders including the archbishop of the Anglican Church of Southern Africa, Thao Makgoba, have signed a letter calling on the British prime minister to help secure a ceasefire in Gaza. The joint letter says that "escalation of war cannot be adequately understood without acknowledging the conflict's broader backdrop—ongoing Israeli occupation and the disenfranchisement of Palestinians for more than 70 years."[62]

CALL FOR CLIMATE FINANCE TO COPE WITH MORE DISASTERS[63]—This is a news item in which Christian Aid wants climate finance for poor countries facing climate disasters. Nushrat Chowdhury, a policy adviser for Christian Aid, said:

> Cyclone Freddy which hit Malawi 2023 was a reminder that communities who have contributed the least to the climate crisis are suffering the worst. Loss and damage costs are in the hundreds of billions of dollars annually in developing countries alone. Wealthy nations must commit the new and additional money required to ensure the Loss and Damage Fund agreed by COP28 can quickly get help to those that need it most.[64]

---

60. *Church Times* 8.12.23, 12.
61. *Church of England Newspaper* 8.12.23, 5.
62. *Church of England Newspaper* 8.12.23, 5.
63. *Church of England Newspaper* 5.1.24, 4.
64. *Church of England Newspaper* 5.1.24, 4.

Non-White Focus in a White County

Typical news items in the category of a **non "race" relations focus in a White country** were as follows:

THOSE MOST DEPRIVED LIVE IN A GOSPEL POVERTY ACCORDING TO MISSION SURVEY[65]—This is report about a mission survey in which a Black actor, Jason Roach, director of ministries at London City Mission, speaks about the proclamation of the Christian gospel in the British context.

> *Everyone needs the opportunity to hear the gospel during their lifetime in a way they can understand. There are millions of people on our doorstep, disconnected from church, who may miss out. The problem is clear, the need to act obvious, but knowing exactly what to do in the heat of the moment can seem daunting and unfamiliar. Christians are willing but need encouragement and strengthening.*[66]

The report seems surprised that those most deprived are less likely to respond to the gospel message. I wonder how serious the writers of this report have considered our Lord's parable of the seed that fell on the roadside and was trampled by the feet of the world. The homeless and refugees are identified as the marginalized in society and unable to hear the gospel, and it would seem that the upwardly mobile have no difficulty in engaging with the Christian faith and sharing its values with others. The news item tells us that the London City Mission has a resource hub for everyday evangelism. It is unclear from the news item what everyday evangelism means—financial aid for the poor or more and better equipped evangelists to tell the poor about the faith. What the news item does tell us is that the Christian faith is being presented in a way that is not meaningful to global majority people.

65. *Church of England Newspaper* 8.12.23, 1.
66. *Church of England Newspaper* 8.12.23, 1.

ACADEMIC BISHOP APPOINTED TO EDMONTON[67]—This news item focuses on the appointment of the Rev. Canon Anderson Jeremiah as bishop of Edmonton in the diocese of London. So what does this news item have to do with our focus on the identification of non-White actors who operate in the context of a White country? When non-White clergy are appointed to senior positions in the Church of England their stories become newsworthy because they allow the institution to claim that there is a significant measure of equality in the appointment system. These stories do not tell us anything about non-White clergy who are British born and reach their glass ceiling during the early days of their ministries.

"Race" Relations Revisited

Typical news items in the category of a **"race" relations focus in a White country** were as follows.

BILL AIMS AT VISAS, NOT DEPORTATIONS CREATE LEGAL PATHWAY FOR ASYLUM-SEEKERS, SAYS FRANCIS-DEHQANI[68]—This news items gives focus to a private members' bill introduced to Parliament by the bishop of Chelmsford. The purpose of the bill is to stop people smuggling and the dangers of crossing the channel in small boats, by offering visas to those who have a strong claim to asylum in the UK. According to Dr. Francis-Dehqani:

> *A visa would last for six months, and visa-holders would have their claims for asylum considered through an accelerated process. I am pleased to bring forward this Private Members' Bill on the introduction of a Humanitarian Visa Scheme, which will provide a much-needed opportunity to*

---

67. *Church of England Newspaper* 5.1.24, 3.
68. *Church Times* 8.12.23, 6.

discuss safe routes into the UK for refugees fleeing conflict, persecution, and disasters.[69]

CHURCH WARNED ON "DARK" IMAGERY[70]—This news item gave focus to a World Council of Churches seminar on "Decolonising Beauty: Mission, gender, racism, and health in the skin-whitening pandemic." Part of this news item found a context in Canada where the anti-racism and equality lead for the United Church of Canada, Adele Halliday, spoke about her experience of whiteness, colonialism and internalized racism.

> Many people around me grew up with understanding imposed from the outside that there was something wrong with the colour of our skin, that to be dark skinned, to be black, is not desirable, and to be light was better. There is nothing wrong with the color of my skin. I can say that loudly and clearly . . . . If we only think about darkness as bad and light as good, that impacts how people think about themselves and treat themselves and desire to be light and white, as opposed to celebrating the way in which God has created them.[71]

STANDING FIRM[72]—This news item stands at the bottom of a much larger piece on Oxfam and their intention to stop banking with Barclays. This comes with a picture of thirteen White people protesting outside Baptist House, the home of the Baptist Mission Society in Didcot, Oxfordshire. This is a protest led by Christian Climate Action. The news item with an identifiable non-White actor seems to have been squeezed in with a photograph of Njie Haddy, who is chair of Inclusive Equal Rights UK. This is interesting because the story here is the campaign to make York the first anti-racist city in the

---

69. *Church Times* 8.12.23, 6.
70. *Church Times* 22/29.12.23, 11.
71. *Church Times* 22/29.12.23, 11.
72. *Church Times* 2.2.24, 6.

north of England, and Njie Haddy is addressing an interfaith and anti-racist summit hosted by the archbishop of York.

HEAVENLY WELCOME FOR REFUGEES IN LIMBO[73]—This is a news item which starts with a story about an asylum seeker who was persecuted in Iran for running an underground church and was rescued by the coast guard in the English Channel. The news item goes on to talk about a drop-in center supported by the local church and has a photograph of the Rev. David Nyirongo with members of the Ukrainian community.

CHURCH LEADERS CRITICISE CLEVERLY REFORMS TO REFUGEE RULES[74]—A news item in which the bishop of Chelmsford, Guli Francis-Dehqani, along with other Church leaders challenge the government's immigration policy to raise the minimum income for family visas to £8,700.

DEBATES ON RACIAL JUSTICE AND SLAVERY TO FEATURE AT GENERAL SYNOD[75]—A news item in which Lord Boateng, chair of the Archbishops' Commission on Racial Justice, challenges the Church of England to stop "marginalizing racial justice concerns" and "relegating it to a secondary issue and the fringes of Synod."[76]

Endnote: Three Decades On, Asking If Anything Has Changed in the Religious Press of the Church of England

As in the first part of this chapter, only a minority of news items were concerned with "race" related issues or contained identifiable non-White actors. However, there was a small percentage increase in both papers for "race" related issues from 3.00 percent to 4.2

---

73. *Church Times* 22/29.12.23, 7.
74. *Church of England Newspaper* 8.12.23, 3.
75. *Church of England Newspaper* 2.2.24, 4.
76. *Church of England Newspaper* 2.2.24, 4.

percent (*The Church Times*) and from 3.4 percent to 5.4 percent (*The Church of England Newspaper*). However, there was a significant increase in the number of news items with identifiable non-White actors in *The Church Times*, going from 5.7 percent to 10.2 percent; *The Church of England Newspaper* remained much the same with a reduction from 9.5 percent to 9.1 percent. So, we can no longer say that the percentage of news items with identifiable non-White actors was greater in *The Church of England Newspaper* than it was in *The Church Times*, as was the case for the 1990–91 sample of newspapers. But what can we say about the percentage of these news items occurring in a "race" relations context? Here we find that *The Church Times* went from 2.7 percent to 6.6 percent while *The Church of England Newspaper* went from the same percentage to 6.1 percent. So we see an increase in news items about "race" relations. So, did these non-White actors appear in a context independent of White people? The answer is no because there was also an increase in the number of news items about non-White issues with no identifiable non-White actors largely in the context of a predominantly non-White country. In both papers there was a neglect of political issues involving non-White people in British society. And when global majority people did appear, they were allowed to speak for themselves when the context was one of a predominantly non-White country. Overall, there was a commonality of racialized framing in *The Church Times* and *The Church of England Newspaper*. People of global majority heritage are excluded by this racialized frame of reference.

So, what of the standard of journalism in the religious press for the contemporary period? On the whole this was generally good and balanced, but this reached an all-time low with a news item in *The Church of England Newspaper* equating anti-Semitism with anti-Zionism, as if they were the same thing.[77] The reporting process failed its readers big time by not providing an alternative view separating these concepts from each other following the position of the US Congress. A news item in *The Church Times* took its lead from the archbishop of Canterbury, who presents Islamophobia and

---

77. *Church of England Newspaper* 8.12.23, 5.

anti-Semitism as if they were interchangeable subjects.[78] The reporting process following Justin Welby's commentary would suggest that racial prejudice and discrimination had somehow been imported into the UK. We are left with the old and familiar idea that Britain as a nation is warm and receptive toward refugees.

---

78. *Church Times* 8.12.23, 10.

Conclusion

The Racialization Process and the Religious Press of the Church of England

I STARTED *FAITH IN Church Newspapers* by talking about my retirement from parochial ministry. It makes every sense to end in the same way. I have been reading Paul Beasley-Murray's book *Make the Most of Retirement*.[1] This writer talks about letting go of past hurts and tries to put this into a theological framework.[2] I am able to go along with some of his practical advice on retirement, but his theology I find questionable. But let's deal with the good stuff first. So how do we deal with our anger, which can be perceived by others as embitterment? So, what is the practice of forgiveness? We start with scripture and Luke 23:34: "Father, forgive them, for they do not know what they are doing." For Beasley-Murray forgiveness is not about providing an excuse for the bishops, archdeacons, and others who have wronged us. To let go and forgive is not to forget

1. Beasley-Murray, *Making the Most*.
2. Beasley-Murray, *Making the Most*, 119–23.

what they did because there are lessons here to be learned. Rather, it means we take the initiative in an ongoing process of liberation from those destructive forces of anger and pain. So, we have to discern what has been going on before it can be addressed. Many of these hurts were shared experiences with my wife, Linda, and she will tell you that some senior office holders are worse than dishonest, they are deceptive because they mean to lie both to themselves and particularly to those of global majority heritage. However, we both feel that this can't be just at a personal level because these hurts are inflicted by the institution. This is where Beasley-Murray's theology falls apart, because Jesus did not die in our place as a punishment for our individual sins. This approach is known by some theologians as penal substitution.[3] As far as Linda and I are concerned, such a theology would make God into the biggest child abuser of all time.

So, did Jesus have to die? And why is Beasley-Murray claiming it was necessary and indeed inevitable?[4] I would argue that if humankind had accepted Jesus' teaching and applied this to the building of a new world, there would have been no necessity for the death of Christ. If we had not fallen from our original innocence into greed and strife, when Christ came as good fruit and symbol of life, we would have accepted both him and his teaching. Jesus died because of our sins, not for them. God did not demand that his Son be offered as a blood sacrifice, but rather that Jesus gave his life as a ransom for many, as a soldier would die for his country. Jesus was prepared to go all the way for us. He came to show us that although we have turned away from God, God has not turned away from us. If there is a barrier between God and us, it is one that we have put there. Once we see that, at our request, God will come and make his home with us, then that barrier falls. But it still remains standing for those who have not eyes to see or ears to hear.

---

3. Isiorho, "Black Identities and Faith Adherence," 283–92.
4. Beasley-Murray, *Making the Most*, 120.

Ambition, Politics, and Church

When I trained for church ministry, many years ago at Westcott House, Cambridge, I knew who the ambitious ones were among my fellow students because they were those who had been to private schools and were less likely to attend local churches on a Sunday morning. They also had private financial means and certainly were not dependent on Church grants. I have seen many of my colleagues get senior jobs in the Church, not because of any obvious ability, but because they know the right people and they have a liking for the power and the prestige that come with those jobs. This is all very well if those leaders used their power and influence for the good of God's people, but sadly I see a lot of selfish ambition in our church, which does nothing for the common good and the building of God's kingdom. I really do feel called to say that as a prophetic act of witness and know it won't be well received in all quarters.

So, is our system of senior appointments corrupt and elitist? This is something I now leave with my readers to discern. There is nothing wrong with looking for and gaining high office, but surely it has got to be for the right reasons. The only good reason to have power in any institution is to use it for radical change. In the United States and many other countries, the bishops are elected by those whom they feel called to serve. To my mind this has got to be better than the system we have here in the UK, which includes government and the Crown, who are involved in the decision-making process. I am sure our Church leadership would look very different if the people in the pew and the local clergy had a say in these decisions.

The Church is often criticized today for interfering in matters which, allegedly, should not concern it. Politicians say we should not concern ourselves with politics even though such issues affect the poor and the powerless in our inner cities and the developing world. And more in the safe and leafy shires whose well-planned pensions or whose high-flying jobs no longer seem so secure. Our critics say we should concentrate on saving people's souls and safeguarding their morality. We are accused in the newspapers and on television of putting forward the view that it does not matter what you do in bed as long as you have the correct political attitude. This is set in opposition to those in our Church who do want to legislate what consenting adults do with each other. We are then accused of being obsessed with sexuality to the exclusion of other aspects of the human condition.

Jesus never took a party-political position, but this did not prevent him from being at the heart of the political and social issues of his day—asking the questions that people would rather he did not ask. Why else did he stir up the power factions of his day so much that they wanted him dead? He was not gentle Jesus meek and mild. This is the Jesus who knows how to kick some ass.[5] Jesus was a powerfully compelling man who was more than capable of taking direct action when it was appropriate to do so. A man who could not help drawing all kinds and conditions of people to his warmth and his loving wholeness. For ourselves, we need to remember that the gospel was written down by people increasingly anxious to survive the hostility of the authorities. Even in that context, the robust, liberation-focused Jesus shines through. As Christians, we must be concerned about all issues of social justice that should engage the human condition. This is God's world and as human beings, we are set in it as stewards, with a mandate to love God and to love our neighbor as ourselves. Our concern should be for the wholeness and fulfillment of all people since all are of equal worth in the love of God. As Christians, we are charged with the responsibility of loving each other and challenging injustice.

. . . .

So how inclusive is the Church of England as a White-majority church? Certainly, the celebration of its diversity can be seen as an expression of Englishness. However, ecclesiastical diversity is not to be confused with cultural inclusiveness. By defining Anglicanism within the English context, we can easily be led to a debate

5. See John 2:13–16.

about the inclusiveness of the methods for interpreting Scripture. But what is the ability of this church to include worshipers from diverse ethnic origins? For the Church of England, racial justice issues still remain controversial and marginalized. *Faith in Church Newspapers* explores the implications for White majority churches in their relationship with people of world majority heritage by demonstrating that the mode of involvement of these churches is driven by a political agenda that has its origin in English ethnicity. *Faith in Church Newspapers* focuses on ethnic inequality and power relationships. These structural inequalities have been racialized and reproduced within the religious press of the Church of England. So, what is *Faith in Church Newspapers* about? This book is not just about the religious press; it is also about the Church of England and its establishment status in English society. It is about racism and colonialism within that institution.

Inclusiveness Issues That Find a Starting Point in John 17

In this conclusion, St. John's Gospel is a starting point that takes us on a journey from the Upper Room to the modern day and to the issues that, as global majority people, we face, especially in my own context, the Church of England. Much of this is further informed by my background as a contextual theologian. I also use semantics to explore some of the pragmatics that cloak injustice within the church.

The setting of John 17 is the Upper Room; the occasion is the last time together for Jesus and his followers before he left for Gethsemane from where he was to be arrested. During his discourse to them, Jesus tried to cover various topics to do with how he and God relate to this world. *Faith in Church Newspapers* makes connections between that discourse and a socio-political understanding of incarnation and crucifixion and relates this to the witness of Black Christians and their theology of context. I draw a distinction between inclusiveness, an approach or attitude toward including people, and inclusivity, which operates at the policy and institutional level. Inclusiveness is a personal characteristic while inclusivity is governed by laws and formally agreed protocols. Readers may find it helpful to use the racism-institutionalized racism paradigm to understand my semantics here.

So how do we do mission and relate this to Christian unity? Many years ago, a reciprocal connection was identified between unity that empowers mission and mission that demonstrates unity. We can locate mission and unity in John 17 as part of Jesus' prayer to his heavenly Father before his arrest in the garden of Gethsemane and his subsequent crucifixion. Our Lord prays for his disciples as the Jesus of history and for all his future disciples as the Christ of faith. He leaves them in no doubt that they will face persecution if they, in following him, challenge and reject the accepted standards of the world.

In John 17, Jesus' earthly work was finished, although he leaves his disciples in the world with work to do as the commissioned body of Christ. Each disciple received their own personal Pentecost moment, echoed to this day in the laying on of hands at ordination and confirmation ceremonies. This has clear implications for us as we engage with the Christ of faith within our own context. It is personal! There are good works for us to walk in which may well remain undone if we do not step up to the mark. The world that hated the Jesus of history would also hate the disciples of faith who are now tasked with the glorification of God on earth by always actively seeking to make the kingdom. Jesus' prayer focused on his request that his disciples would have the strength to complete their mission in the world even if they, or we, would prefer to be with their Lord in heaven. There can be therefore no triumphalism in this schema. We are called to act and to do a mission right here and now. This earth-bound strengthening amounts to a consecration, setting the disciples, and in succession us, apart to realize a vision of the truth about God in Christ Jesus. Through the incarnation, God has entered into an eternal contract with us which sees the crucifixion as a public act of rescue, an indelible marker on time of the eternal love of God in Christ Jesus.

The work of the kingdom will only be completed with the universal acceptance of God's glory as seen in the loving unity of Jesus' disciples so that they "may be one" as he and his Father were one. The Jesus of history and Christ of faith are united in this compelling picture of the church presented to the world. We have actually very few commandments given to us by Jesus. Jesus summed up all the law in the two great dominical commandments: Love God and love your neighbors. This is at the same time simple and profoundly complicated. If we look at these two commands, then we find three concepts that are at the heart of the Christian faith: love, God, and our neighbors, locked into a sense of the other. These are not self-explanatory. How do we sharpen this understanding? Who are my neighbors? Who am I? What is a person? These questions are all intricately linked, and every culture has a different take on their answers.

The irresistible image of loving unity contained in John 17 is the vision of God's truth reflected in the world bringing us closer to God and to each other as we try to love our neighbor as ourselves. Interesting concept in an age where self-loathing and the relentless drive to improve by changing are dominant themes in the advertising and other popular media. Giving expression to this unity in our own theology of context is to see the compassion of Christ in our neighbors. But who are our neighbors and what do they look like? From a Black perspective, some of our neighbors are White.

In our Western culture we tend to think of ourselves as being composed of mind and body, visible and invisible, all very post platonic. We feel that what endures after death is the mind or spirit part of ourselves and that our bodies perish. So, we are split, dichotomized, and our two halves do not always get on well together. We also see ourselves as distinct and separate entities who can lose touch with ourselves if we deny ourselves the right to self-expression. If I said that I was seeking to understand my own identity, then you would know exactly what I meant.

In God, all our barriers are broken down and a type of unity both terrifying and beautiful is ushered in. In God, cause and effect are brought together in a way that invites us to take some true control. For if we truly take on board the idea of *neighbor* then no one is a distant entity anymore. Everyone becomes an intimate part of our own selves because we are caught up equally in the redeeming and suffering love of God. I cannot become a cruel person and exploit others in obvious or subtle ways because what I do to the least of these my kinsfolk, I know I do to God, who is our ultimate kinsperson.

I cannot alienate another person and regard them as less human than I am because I know that they are, as I am, made in the image of God and redeemed in the blood of our dear Lord. And this is where at last we begin to find an answer to our question: Who is my neighbor? For if we are each of us doubly a reflection of the divine reality, being made by God and rescued through Christ, then my neighbor is precious. Until I treat my neighbor with all the respect that I know I should give them, then I am denying the image of God within them. We must seek to discover the divinity within each person. The churches should take stock of how they regard people and what expectations they have of their treatment and of their status within society, which is the province of inclusivity. We must look into the eyes of those who share the world with us and remember what else they share. They share a birthright in the effective and transforming love of God.

John 17 deals with the ultimate victory of God over the world. The followers now feel that, at last, they have begun to understand what Jesus has been trying to tell them. Jesus warns them that they are about to leave him all alone. The theme of betrayal is continued. In Jesus, we are sent the actuality of what it means for God to be loving and patient; God who is passionately bonded to humanity. God's judgment burns with the fierce flame of perfect justice, but God's compassion extends to us the means of surviving that judgment. God's love is all the more terrifying because we see ourselves as we are within its clarity.

The theme of going to the Father does not go far enough in giving us an idea of either the close intertwining between God and ourselves or of the intimate connection between the Creator and the

Redeemer. After all, in terms of the physical reality, a father can be someone all too sadly distant from any offspring. Of course, many fathers are kindly disposed to their children. How many times do we say the Lord's Prayer without a thought about the almost incredible assertion that it starts with "Our Father"?

So, what has all this got to do with church newspapers? And what was this book about? I am asking crucial questions about inclusiveness and exclusivity issues that find a starting point in John 17 but can be concluded in an understanding of the racialization process that operates not just in the religious press of the Church of England but in the established Church. *Faith in Church Newspapers* is concerned both with the findings from the analysis of these papers (chapter 4) and with the wider implications for Christian mission in the Church of England. My introduction sets out the methodological structure for making sense of news items in *The Church Times* and *The Church of England Newspaper*. Chapter 1 focused on identifiable and identified case studies in global majority heritage. I tried to give the reader insight into who these people are behind the quantifiable statistics about newspaper coverage. Chapter 2—"'Race' Related Issues and Their Theology of Context"—was a substantial chapter that focused on Church reports about inter-cities and the social enterprise agenda. The urban cities and large towns are where most Black and Asian people live in the UK, and it is in this context they are subject to economic and social deprivation. When I got to the end of chapter 4, I wanted to know if anything had changed in the religious press of the Church of England. The conclusions here are drawn from that data and tell us things about the Church of England as much as they do about the religious press.

The religious press of the Church of England understands the presence of people from global majority heritage as within a "race" relations problematic. This approach is initially about the characteristics of those who are defined as belonging to "races" and the politics between them. It is also about the so-called host society that does not always know whether it wants to engage with so-called ethnic minorities or to exclude them. The focus is on the Black worshipers and their lowly place in the White institution which forms the nature of the immigrant-host relationship. This approach does not ask questions about racism, racialized relations, and the attitudes, actions, and motivations of White worshipers who collectively have the power to exclude those they perceive as different from themselves. This obscures the potential impact of multiple variables that are involved in the racialization process. This leads us to ask how the "race" relations process is constructed that attributes meaning to previously racially unclassified relationships. And what about religious behavior within this context?

. . . .

So why have I raised these questions? And what are the implications for the reporting process of Church newspapers and identifiable non-White actors? And what is the context in which the reporting process takes place? If the Church of England is mission-shaped it ought to have something to say to Black and Asian Christians, the majority of whom worship in urban locations, often supporting congregations far larger than their White counterparts. So how has the Church and the religious press avoided any serious discussion of either Black theology or antiracism as a vital concern of all Christians and in particular those living in the inner city? However, that brings us to questions that are even more important. Is there to be any joined-up writing between Church reports, multiple policy committees on every subject under the sun, and a new strategic framework at least every five years, or do they all hold their territory with little or no communication between them? Why are the needs of marginalized groups not given center stage in the mainstream arena of the Church of England? The answer would seem to be that they are marginalized by definition and as such are unlikely to get any consideration outside of their own prescribed area.

This brings us to the Church of England report *From Lament to Action*.[6] The report is not optimistic about its possible impact

6. Archbishop's Anti-Racist Taskforce, *From Lament to Action*.

on the institution it seeks to challenge. *From Lament to Action* shares with its readers the idea that history could repeat itself and that this report will be ignored by the Church of England along with all the other reports on racism during the last twenty-five years. The report called for the funding of a racial justice officer in each of the forty-four dioceses of the Church of England. This was rejected by the General Synod. So, the best we can hope for will be an allocation of money to employ a handful of specialist officers on short-term contracts in those dioceses where the institutional Church cannot deny there are a considerable number of so-called ethnic minority people. *From Lament to Action* wants an annual report in which to blame and shame those responsible for denying racial justice in the appointment system of the Church. This presupposes that the institutions and the individuals involved have shame to blame. For many years, these bodies have failed to provide diverse shortlists that could lead to the appointment of people of global majority heritage to senior posts. The Church of England remains an institutionally racially biased organization. So, to deliver even in a partial way on some of the recommendations of *From Lament to Action* would seriously challenge the ethos and culture of the Church of England.

So where do we need to be? How do we get there via a mission-shaped Church that does not recognize its global majority heritage members though its religious press? Are the "Who are we" questions about Church identity or self-knowledge? Does our understanding of Mother Church keep the *we-ness* in our common enterprise? What is the interplay between faith, devotion, teaching and outreach, and building, as we consider new patterns of ministry? How do we keep the Church, break down barriers, and reach into the world? I will answer the last questions by saying that we can do this only by recapturing the early church models of inclusive ministries, driven as they were by the urgency of the parousia and by the promptings of love.